Edexcel GCSE (9-1) 1CP2
Computer Science

P.M. Heathcote

S. Robson

Published by
PG Online Limited
The Old Coach House
35 Main Road
Tolpuddle
Dorset
DT2 7EW
United Kingdom
sales@pgonline.co.uk
www.pgonline.co.uk
2024

PG ONLINE

Acknowledgements

The answers in the Teacher's Supplement are the sole responsibility of the authors and have neither been provided nor approved by the examination boards.

We would also like to thank the following for permission to reproduce copyright photographs:

Page 2: London Underground passengers photo © Matthew Ashmore

Page 2: Angel of the North © Ron Ellis / Shutterstock

Page 4: London Underground map © Thinglass / Shutterstock.com

Color Picker screenshot © Adobe Inc.

Other photographic images © Shutterstock

Cover picture: 'Antibes' 2017
Acrylic on linen, 100 cm x 100 cm
© Deborah Lanyon
www.deborahlanyon.co.uk

Cover artwork, graphics and typesetting by PG Online Ltd

First edition 2024 10 9 8 7 6 5 4 3 2 1

A catalogue entry for this book is available from the British Library

ISBN: 978-1-916518-14-8

Copyright © P.M. Heathcote, S. Robson, PG Online 2024

Editor: J Franklin

This product is made of material from well-managed FSC® certified forests and from recycled materials.

Printed by Bell & Bain Ltd, Glasgow, UK.

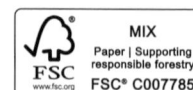

FSC
MIX
Paper | Supporting responsible forestry
www.fsc.org FSC® C007785

Preface

Aimed at GCSE students, this book provides comprehensive yet concise coverage of all the topics covered in the Edexcel GCSE (9-1) Computer Science (1CP2) specification, written and presented in a way that is accessible to teenagers. It can be used as a course text and as assessment preparation for students nearing the end of their course.

It is divided into seven sections covering every element of the specification. Sections 6A and 6B of the textbook cover programming concepts with a practical approach to provide students with experience of understanding, writing and adapting programs that solve problems.

Each chapter contains exercises and exam-style questions. Answers to all of these are available to teachers only in a free Teachers' Supplement which can be ordered from our website **www.pgonline.co.uk**.

Endorsement Statement

In order to ensure that this resource offers high-quality support for the associated Pearson qualification, it has been through a review process by the awarding body. This process confirms that this resource fully covers the teaching and learning content of the specification or part of a specification at which it is aimed. It also confirms that it demonstrates an appropriate balance between the development of subject skills, knowledge and understanding, in addition to preparation for assessment.

Endorsement does not cover any guidance on assessment activities or processes (e.g. practice questions or advice on how to answer assessment questions), included in the resource nor does it prescribe any particular approach to the teaching or delivery of a related course.

While the publishers have made every attempt to ensure that advice on the qualification and its assessment is accurate, the official specification and associated assessment guidance materials are the only authoritative source of information and should always be referred to for definitive guidance.

Pearson examiners have not contributed to any sections in this resource relevant to examination papers for which they have responsibility.

Examiners will not use endorsed resources as a source of material for any assessment set by Pearson.

Endorsement of a resource does not mean that the resource is required to achieve this Pearson qualification, nor does it mean that it is the only suitable material available to support the qualification, and any resource lists produced by the awarding body shall include this and other appropriate resources.

This resource was designed using the most up to date information from the specification. Specifications are updated over time which means there may be contradictions between the resource and the specification, therefore please use the information on the latest specification and Sample Assessment Materials at all times when ensuring students are fully prepared for their assessments.

Contents

Paper 1 – Computer systems

Edexcel GCSE 1CP2 (9-1) Specification map

		Section 1	Section 2	Section 3	Section 4	Section 5	Section 6A & 6B
1	**Computational thinking**						
1.1	Decomposition and abstraction	✓					
1.2	Algorithms	✓					
1.3	Truth tables	✓					
2	**Data**						
2.1	Binary		✓				
2.2	Data representation		✓				
2.3	Data storage		✓				
3	**Computers**						
3.1	Hardware			✓			
3.2	Software			✓			
3.3	Programming languages			✓			
4	**Networks**						
4.1	Networks				✓		
4.2	Network security				✓		
5	**Issues and impact**						
5.1	Environmental					✓	
5.2	Ethical and legal					✓	
5.3	Cybersecurity					✓	
6	**Programming**						
6.1	Develop code						✓
6.2	Constructs						✓
6.3	Data types and structures						✓
6.4	Input/output						✓
6.5	Operators						✓
6.4	Subprograms						✓

Section 1

Computational thinking

Objectives

- understand the benefit of using decomposition and abstraction to model aspects of the real world and analyse, understand and solve problems
- understand the benefits of using subprograms
- be able to follow and write algorithms including flowcharts, pseudocode and program code
- be able to use sequence, selection and repetition
- know how to use both count-controlled and condition-controlled repetition
- be able to use iteration over every item in a data structure
- be able to use input, processing and output to solve problems
- understand how to follow and write algorithms that use variables and constants
- be able to use one- and two-dimensional data structures, including strings, records and arrays
- be able to follow and write algorithms that use the arithmetic operators addition, subtraction, division, multiplication, modulus, integer division and exponentiation
- understand how to follow and write algorithms that use the relational operators equal to, less than, greater than, not equal to, less than or equal to, greater than or equal to
- be able to follow and write algorithms that use the logical operators AND, OR and NOT
- determine the correct output of an algorithm for a given set of data
- be able to use a trace table to determine the value variables will hold at a given point in an algorithm
- understand the errors that occur in programs including syntax, logic and runtime
- be able to identify and correct logic errors in algorithms
- understand how the linear search and binary search algorithms work
- understand how the bubble sort and merge sort algorithms work
- be able to use logical reasoning and test data to evaluate an algorithm's fitness for purpose and efficiency
- understand that efficiency may be considered in terms of the number of comparisons, number of passes through a loop or the use of memory
- be able to apply the logical operators AND, OR and NOT in truth tables with up to three inputs to solve problems

1.1 – Algorithms, decomposition and abstraction

Computational thinking

Computer Science is all about studying problems and working out how to solve them. The problem might be a mathematical one such as adding the numbers 1 to 100, or finding all the prime numbers less than a million. It might be something less well-defined, such as getting a computer to recognise when the platform of an underground railway is becoming dangerously full. It could be a problem that a virus-checker attempts to solve – detecting when your computer has a virus.

A human being looking at a CCTV of an underground platform would be able to tell quite easily if it was too crowded, and no more people should be allowed through the barrier, but how do we get a computer to recognise that situation?

Some of the key concepts in computational thinking include:

- abstraction
- decomposition
- algorithmic thinking

Abstraction

Abstraction involves removing unnecessary details from a problem in order to solve it. We are all familiar with the idea of abstracting away details from abstract paintings and statues; think of the famous statue 'Angel of the North' by Antony Gormley, dominating the skyline near the A1 at Gateshead.

How can this principle be applied to the problem of recognising a crowded platform? The computer needs to pick out the relevant objects and ignore the rest. It can ignore the background lights, the colour of the clothes people are wearing, whether they are carrying rucksacks and whether they are male or female. The only important fact is how many heads can be detected.

> **Q1** Consider other ways a computer could work out whether a platform is overcrowded? Is the presence of the train relevant?

Abstraction is used in thousands of different ways to aid in problem-solving. One common method of problem-solving is by using simulation – building a model of a problem and finding out what happens under different circumstances. Of course, it does not have to be a physical model; it is more likely to be what is termed a 'logical' model, that is, one which describes the basic facts and performs multiple calculations to help predict what will happen in different circumstances. Simulations of this sort include:

- weather forecast models
- financial models such as economic forecasts for governments or tools to calculate whether your business is likely to make a profit
- population models to help predict the likely population in 20 years' time, based on current trends
- queueing models, to help estimate how many toll-booths will be needed on a new motorway, or how many checkouts there need to be in a new supermarket

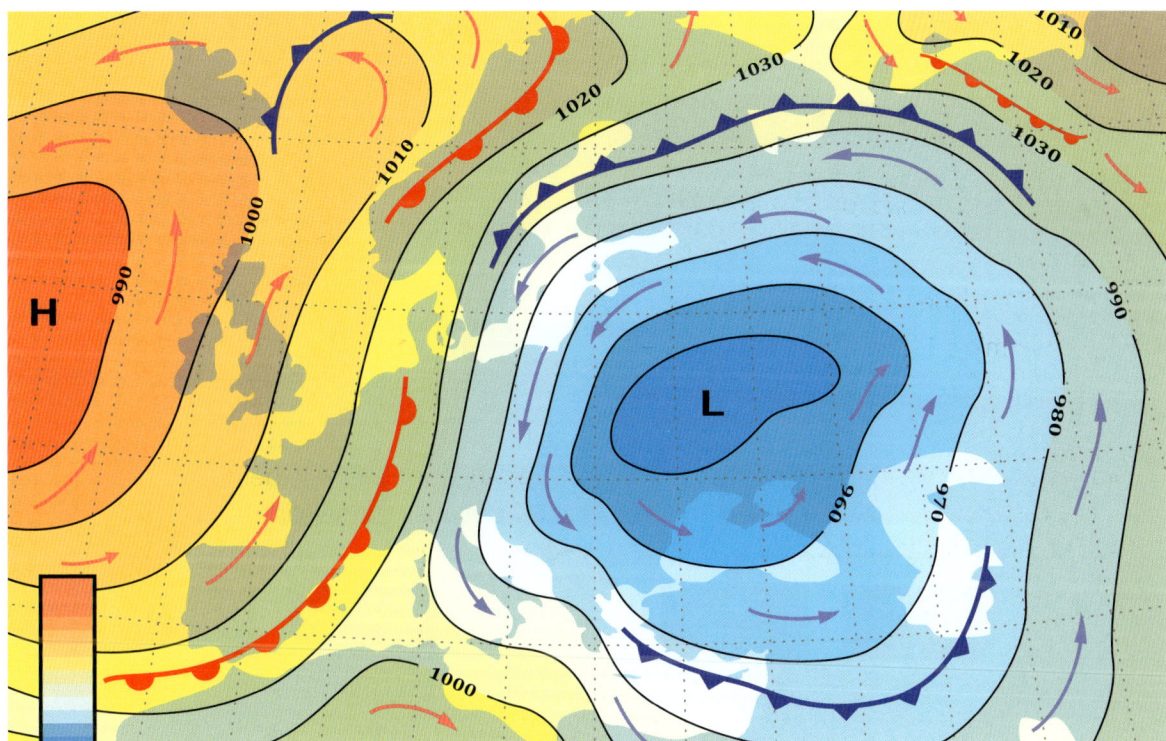

> **Q2** What would be the inputs to each of these models? How is abstraction used in each case?

Abstraction allows us to separate the 'logical' from the 'physical'. A good example of this is the map of the London Underground – all we need to know is what stations are on which line, and the best route to get from A to B. There is no need to be concerned by the details of the exact distance between stations or even in which direction the route actually takes us at any given moment.

Similarly, we are all quite happy to use a computer or drive a car without having much idea of how it works. A driver, a child in the back seat and a mechanic all have a very different view of a car. We abstract away everything we don't need to know about and concentrate on the essentials.

Decomposition

When you start programming, the whole program fits on the screen. It is really easy to see what is happening and fix the problems. As programs get much bigger they become unmanageable so we need to break them into smaller sections.

Decomposition involves breaking down a problem into smaller, simpler steps or stages. For example, imagine we are writing a computer game which has many complex levels. We could break it up as follows:

Each of the boxes could be further sub-divided until each box represents a single, simple sub-task. When tasks are broken down in this way, i.e. decomposed, it becomes much easier to solve the problem. Each small part of it is itself a small, manageable subproblem for which the steps in a solution can be written down.

Benefits of using subprograms

Large programs become unmanageable and difficult for programmers to find errors in.

By using decomposition to break a problem down, smaller mini programs called subprograms can be created. For instance, in a computer game, the following screen would be difficult to create by programming all the different components in a single program.

Instead, subprograms could be created such as:

- Display Lives
- Display Message
- Display Background
- Display Score

The main program can now make use of these subprograms to build the screen.

The benefits of using subprograms are:

- It makes fixing errors easier
- If an error is fixed in a subprogram, it will be fixed everywhere in the program that uses it
- Each individual subprogram can be tested on its own
- Subprograms can be reused in other programs

What is an algorithm?

An algorithm is a series of steps that can be followed to complete a task. It is not the same thing as a computer program – before you can write the program you have to work out the steps needed to solve the given problem. Writing the code is the easy part; working out exactly what the code has to do is more difficult. The way programmers consider how they will solve problems is known as **algorithmic thinking**.

A working algorithm will always finish and return an answer or perform the task it was supposed to. "Always finishes" is something you may take for granted until you write a program that gets stuck in an infinite loop (always save before you run your program).

Let's take a step back from programming for a moment. Other sorts of algorithm that you may be familiar with are:

- recipes
- directions
- instructions to build a Lego® model
- instructions for flat-pack furniture

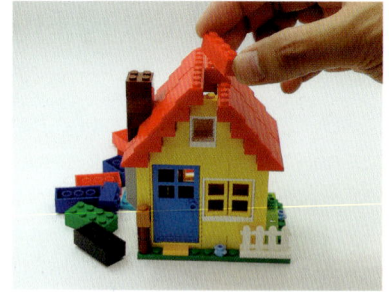

Here's a problem:

How do I get from the Winchester service station on the M3 to Winchester High Street?

An algorithm does not have to be written in code. The first steps to working out the design will be to draw diagrams and/or list the steps involved.

We will be looking at how to break down the problem and then structure a solution using some standard tools called flowcharts and pseudocode.

Only when the solution has some structure can you effectively start coding it. Pseudocode is the first step to actual code as it outlines the algorithm in programming constructs but doesn't rely on any specific language syntax.

1

Winchester Services
Shroner Wood, Winchester SO21 1PP, United Kingdom

> Get on M3

3 min (0.4 mi)

> Follow M3 to A272. Take exit 9 from M3

4 min (3.6 mi)

⌄ Continue on A272. Take A31 to B3330

7 min (2.7 mi)

○ At the roundabout, take the 1st exit onto A272

0.9 mi

○ At the roundabout, take the 2nd exit onto A31

0.6 mi

○ At the roundabout, take the 1st exit and stay on A31

0.3 mi

○ At the roundabout, take the 2nd exit onto Bar End Rd/B3330
ⓘ Continue to follow Bar End Rd

0.3 mi

↱ Turn right onto Bar End Rd/B3330
ⓘ Continue to follow B3330
ⓘ Go through 1 roundabout

0.5 mi

○ At the roundabout, take the 1st exit onto Bridge St/B3330
ⓘ Continue to follow B3330

364 ft

High St
Winchester SO23, UK

Q3 Look at the following algorithm:

```
x = 0
FOR n = 1 TO 10
        ask user to enter a mark
        accept the mark
        IF mark > x THEN
            x = mark
        ENDIF
    ENDFOR
    PRINT(x)
```

What does this algorithm display if the numbers 14, 7, 16, 12, 10, 18, 12, 9, 11, 8 are entered?

What would make this algorithm easier to understand?

1.2 – Developing algorithms using flowcharts

In computing, we write programs or create computer systems to 'solve a problem'. The problem is the need or requirement we have to meet. The solution could be a simple program but is more likely to be a complex suite of hardware and software in a real-world scenario, which will need to be broken down into many programs and subprograms.

Understanding how to solve a problem is important. You cannot just start coding at line 1 and hope to get a working solution straight away. The first step is to write an **algorithm** – that is, the series of steps needed to solve the problem.

This section will consider how algorithms are developed with the aid of **flowcharts** and **pseudocode**. Flowcharts are diagrams which use certain symbols to show the flow of data, processing and input/output taking place in a program or task.

Standard flowchart symbols

This is a **terminator** symbol.

This is used to START and END the flowchart.

This is a **process** symbol. For example:

```
count = count + 1 or total = (a * b) + 3
```

This is an **input/output** symbol. For example:

```
INPUT number or OUTPUT total
```

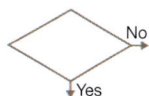

This is a **decision** symbol that can only accept "yes" or "no" answers, for example: `"Is number less than 0?"`

Arrows are used to show the logical flow of the program

This is a **pre-defined subprogram** symbol. For example:

```
calculateAverage(5,10,15)
findCircleArea(radius)
```

Example 1

In this flowchart, the value called `number` is continuously multiplied by 2 and the value is added to `sum` after each iteration of the loop.

The loop continues until the value of `sum` exceeds 29; at this point, `sum` is output.

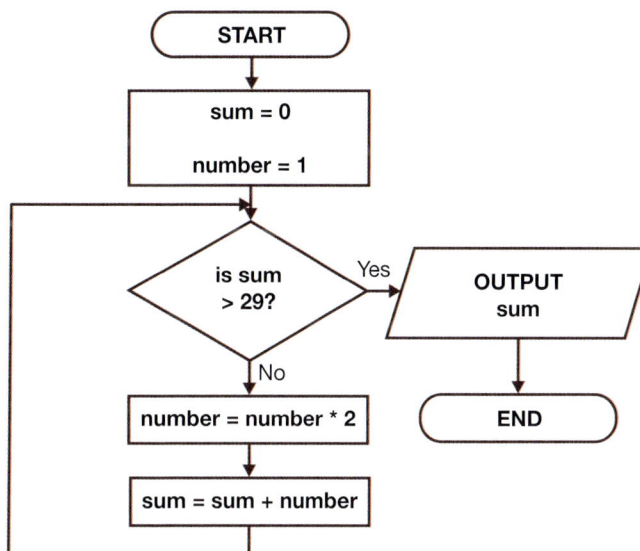

Q4 Complete the trace table for the flowchart on page 7 to show how `sum` and `number` increase. What is output by the algorithm?

number	sum	sum > 29?
1	0	No

Q5 The following flowchart inputs 365 temperatures and outputs the number of days when the temperature was more than 20°C and the number of days when the temperature was below 15°C. The average temperature for the 365 days is also output. Give the statements that need to be inserted at A, B, C and D.

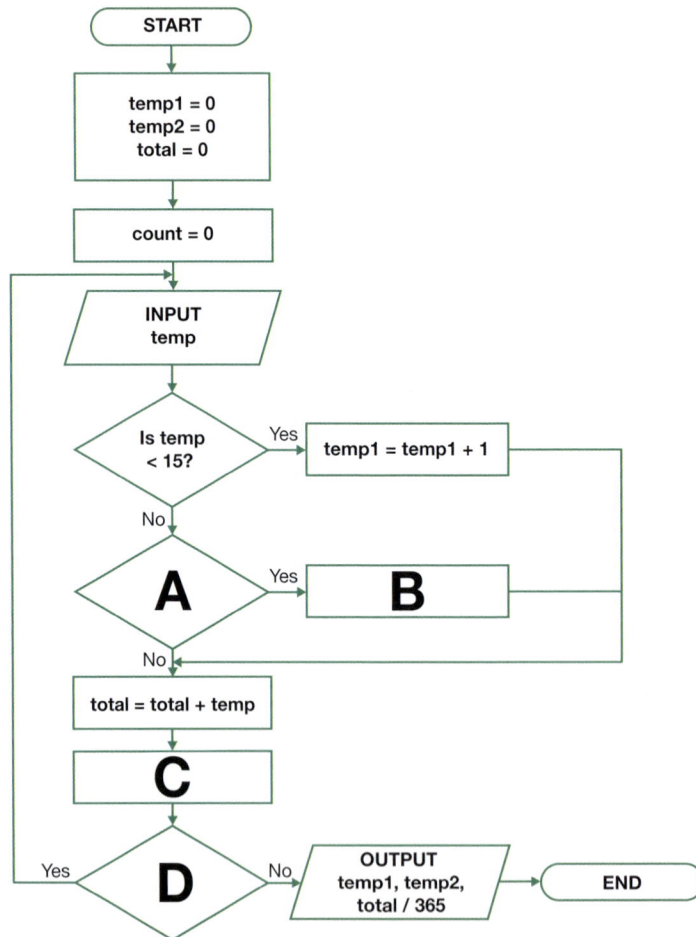

1

```
                    START
                      │
                      ▼
              ┌───────────────┐
              │  temp1 = 0    │
              │  temp2 = 0    │
              │  total = 0    │
              └───────────────┘
                      │
                      ▼
              ┌───────────────┐
              │   count = 0   │
              └───────────────┘
                      │
                      ▼
              ┌───────────────┐
              │     INPUT     │
              │     temp      │
              └───────────────┘
                      │
                      ▼
                 ╱─────────╲      Yes   ┌─────────────────┐
                ╱  Is temp  ╲──────────▶│ temp1 = temp1 + 1│
                ╲  < 15?    ╱           └─────────────────┘
                 ╲─────────╱
                      │ No
                      ▼
                 ╱─────────╲      Yes   ┌─────────────────┐
                ╱    A      ╲──────────▶│        B        │
                ╲           ╱           └─────────────────┘
                 ╲─────────╱
                      │ No
                      ▼
              ┌────────────────────┐
              │ total = total + temp│
              └────────────────────┘
                      │
                      ▼
              ┌───────────────┐
              │       C       │
              └───────────────┘
                      │
                      ▼
         Yes    ╱─────────╲    No    ┌─────────────────┐      ┌──────┐
        ◀──────╱    D      ╲────────▶│     OUTPUT      │─────▶│ END  │
               ╲           ╱         │ temp1, temp2,   │      └──────┘
                ╲─────────╱          │  total / 365    │
                                     └─────────────────┘
```

Q6 Draw a flowchart which inputs the top speed of a number of cars (-1 is used to stop the input). The average top speed of all the cars is finally output.

Q7 Draw a flowchart which outputs the maximum of 10 numbers input by the user.

1.3 – Developing algorithms using pseudocode

Pseudocode is used to write an algorithm in programming-style constructs but it is not in an actual programming language. It is an informal written description of a program that uses English language statements. You do not need to worry about the detailed syntax or be precise about how the code will do something; you just describe the steps you will need in your algorithm.

Basic programming constructs

There are three key constructs used to write algorithms in pseudocode (and in actual code):

- sequence
- selection
- repetition / iteration

Sequence

Sequence is just a matter of writing steps down in the order they need to happen. For example:

```
Input the product price
Input the quantity
Calculate total = quantity x price
Output "Total price is ", total
```

The statements above explain how this algorithm works. In an exam you will see more standardised pseudocode statements used, and the four statements above would be written as:

```
productPrice = USERINPUT
quantity = USERINPUT
total = quantity * price
OUTPUT "Total price is ", total
```

Examples of pseudocode variables, constants and assignment statements

Single values, such as `name` or `costPrice` are stored in **variables** (if the value will change when the program is running) or **constants** (if the value is the same throughout the program).

```
costPrice = 10.0
total = costPrice * 2
gender = "M"
name = "Mike"
option = True


PI = 3.14
MIN_PLAYERS = 2
```

Variable and constant names must be written without spaces. For variable names, two words can be combined using uppercase and lowercase letters, such as `costPrice`. Constants are usually written using just uppercase letters. In this case, words are separated using an underscore (_) character, such as `MIN_PLAYERS`.

1

Selection

Using an IF…THEN…ELSE statement

The IF…THEN…ELSE construct allows you to choose between two options.

```
IF x <= 10 THEN
   z = z + 10
ELSE
   z = z - 10
   y = y + 1
ENDIF
```

Using an IF…THEN statement

You can write an IF…THEN statement without an ELSE.

```
IF gameLevel == 2 THEN
   (instructions here)
ENDIF
```

Notice that the == means equals. This is because = is used for assigning a value to a variable.

Using an IF…ELSE IF statement

```
IF menuChoice == 1 THEN
   display rules
ELSE IF menuChoice == 2 THEN
   play game
ELSE IF menuChoice == 3 THEN
   Exit
ENDIF
```

Nested selection statements

You can also write one or more IF statements nested inside another selection statement. The following example uses a nested IF statement.

Example 1

Write an algorithm to input a username and check if it is equal to MANH123. If it is, input a user password, and check if the password is equal to XYZ123a, otherwise output a message "Invalid username". If the password is correct, output "Access granted", otherwise, output a message "Invalid password".

```
username = USERINPUT
IF username = "MANH123" THEN
   password = USERINPUT
   IF password == "XYZ123a" THEN
     OUTPUT "Access granted"
   ELSE
     OUTPUT "Invalid password"
   ENDIF
ELSE
   OUTPUT "Invalid username"
ENDIF
(continue)
```

Q8 Complete the nested IF statement below to check whether a variable called `element` is in either or both of two lists called `listA` and `listB`, and output an appropriate message.

```
IF element in listA THEN
    IF element in listB THEN
        OUTPUT "Element is in both lists"
    ELSE
        OUTPUT "Element is in List A"
    ENDIF
ELSE
    (insert statements here)
    …
```

Repetition and iteration

Repetition and iteration are similar terms for repeating a section of a program. There are three different types of repetition and iteration that you need to be aware of.

WHILE loop

A WHILE loop is a **condition-controlled** loop. This means that a condition is given at the start of the loop. If the condition is true then the code is repeated. If the condition is false then the loop finishes and the code beneath it is run. The code will execute zero, one or more times depending on the condition.

```
x = USERINPUT
WHILE x != "End"
  OUTPUT x
  x = USERINPUT
ENDWHILE
```

If the user inputs `"End"` before the `WHILE` statement, the loop will not be performed at all and execution will skip to the next statement after the `ENDWHILE` statement. The `!=` in the code above means not equal to.

FOR loop

The FOR loop is a **count-controlled** loop. It allows you to execute a block of code a specific number of times.

```
FOR count = 1 TO 10
  OUTPUT count * 3
ENDFOR
```

Iteration across a data structure

It is also possible to iterate across all items in a data structure such as a list.

```
total = 0
prices = [15, 16, 14, 15, 15, 16]
FOR price in prices
  total = total + price
ENDFOR
OUTPUT total
```

The data structure used here is a list. You need to also understand 2D lists, arrays, strings and records. These are covered in **section 6A**.

Example 2

A computerised form prompts a user to enter their email address.

The validation rules check if the address has an @ symbol in it. If it doesn't, an error message is displayed, the text box is cleared and the system asks the user to enter the email address again. This continues until an appropriate address is entered.

The system then checks that the email address has been typed in lowercase and if not, it converts it to lowercase. Once the email address is ok it is stored in the customer database.

The flowchart and pseudocode for this could be as follows:

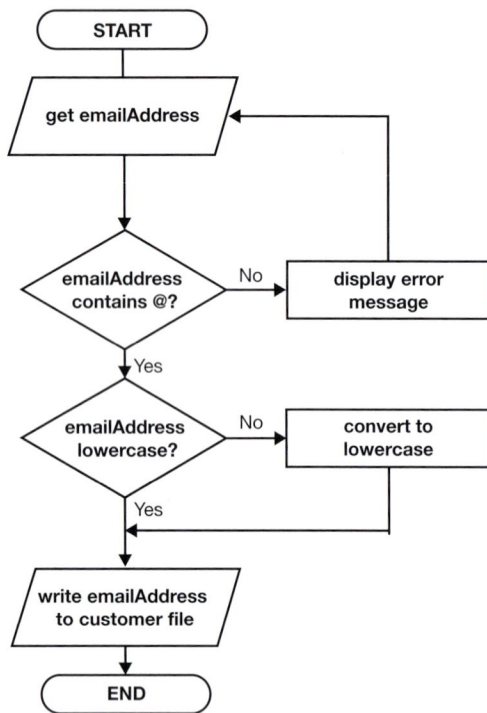

1

```
emailAddress = USERINPUT
WHILE NOT hasAtSign
      OUTPUT error message
      emailAddress = USERINPUT
ENDWHILE
IF emailAddress is not lowercase THEN
      Convert to lowercase
ENDIF

write emailAddress to customer file
```

The line of code `WHILE NOT hasAtSign` will check if `emailAddress` doesn't contain an @ symbol.

Q9 The IF statement to check whether the address is lowercase is not needed. Modify the algorithm so that it performs the same task without using an IF statement.

Q10 Write a pseudocode algorithm which inputs 10 numbers. Each time a number less than zero is input, display which number in the input sequence it is, and its value. When all numbers have been input, display the average of all the negative numbers. Your algorithm should allow for the fact that there may be no negative numbers.

Sample output could be, for example

```
Number 3  -8
Number 7  -20
Average of negative numbers = -14
```

Q11 Write a routine that inputs a series of numbers. Output how many numbers are greater than 60. A dummy value of -1 ends the input.

Conditions

Both `IF` statements and `WHILE` loops make use of conditions. For example:

```
IF <condition> THEN
   DO THESE INSTRUCTIONS
ENDIF
```

The conditions can make use of the relational operators as shown in the table below:

Relational operator	Symbol used
Equal to	==
Not equal to	!=
Less than	<
Less than or equal to	<=
Greater than	>
Greater than or equal to	>=

Conditions can also use the **logical operators** `AND`, `OR` and `NOT`.

For example, a condition in an `IF` statement could be:

```
IF score >= 80 AND timeSpent < 60 THEN
   ADD TO HIGH SCORE TABLE
ENDIF
```

Arithmetic operators

Arithmetic operators are used in the same way as they are in Maths. However, different symbols are often used to make them easier to enter with a keyboard.

Arithmetic operator	Symbol used
Addition	+
Subtraction	-
Division	/
Multiplication	*
Modulus (finding the remainder after division)	%
Integer division (the result of division without the remainder)	//
Exponentiation (to the power of)	**

For example:

a = 60 * 2   (The variable a will store 120 as this is the result of 60 × 2)

b = 15 % 4   (The variable b will store 3 as this is the remainder of 15 ÷ 4)

> **Q12** A computer game allows a player to progress to the next level if they have a score of at least 100 and they have one or more lives.
>
> The pseudocode to complete this has been partially completed below.
> ```
>        IF <condition> THEN
>            PLAY NEXT LEVEL
>        ENDIF
> ```
> Write pseudocode for the condition needed in the pseudocode.

1

Q13 Write the values stored in the following variables once the calculations have been executed.

(a) a = 5 + 7

(b) b = 70 / 100

(c) c = 12 % 5

(d) d = 21 // 5

(e) e = 5**2

Types of errors

When programming, it is possible that an error is made. There are three different types of error that occur.

Error type	Cause	Examples

Syntax error	The programmer has made a mistake in the syntax of their program. For example, they may have misspelt a keyword or put some symbols in the wrong order.	```print("Hello)```
		```prnt("Hello")```
		```print("Hello"```

Logic error	The program will run, but it won't work in the way that the programmer intended.	```a = 10```
		```b = 20```
		```average = (a + b) / 3```

Runtime error	An error will occur whilst the program is running.	```a = 10```
		```b = 0```
		```c = a / b```

Q14 Three syntax errors are given in the table above. Explain the error for each one.

Q15 One logic error and one runtime error are given in the table above. Explain the error that has occurred for each one.

1.4 – Searching algorithms

Before starting to write original algorithms to solve problems, it is worth considering some well-known algorithms for searching and sorting. These are operations that are frequently needed in real world programs.

Thousands of software applications, including databases or commercial search engines such as Google, depend on the ability to quickly search through huge amounts of data to find a particular item.

Q16 Name some other organisations that store huge amounts of data which often need to be searched quickly to find a particular item.

We are going to consider two search algorithms in this section. Two of the most common search routines are:

- Linear search
- Binary search

A linear search

When data is unsorted, the only sensible option when searching for a particular item is to start at the beginning and look at every item until you find the one you want. You could be lucky and find the item quite quickly if it's near the beginning of the list, or you could be unlucky and find it right at the end of the list.

Q17 If you have a list of 10,000 unsorted names, on average how many items will need to be examined until you find the one you are looking for?

Here is an algorithm for a linear search:

```
1.  found = False
2.  Start at the first name
3.  REPEAT
4.    Examine the current name in the list
5.    IF it's the one you are looking for THEN
6.      found = True
7.    ENDIF
8.  UNTIL found = True OR reach end of list
9.  IF found = True THEN
10.   OUTPUT name
11. ELSE
12.   OUTPUT "Not found"
13. ENDIF
```

The algorithm as written is a long way from something you can turn into program code, but it describes how you might go about solving the problem.

Example 3

Look at the following list of integers:

14	2	3	11	1	9	5	8	10	6

The items you would examine to find the number **5** would be: **14, 2, 3, 11, 1, 9, 5**

Q18 Write down the items you would examine to locate the item with value 7 in the above list.

A binary search

If the list is sorted, (i.e. in numerical or alphabetical order), you can use a much more efficient algorithm called a binary search. It works by repeatedly dividing in half the portion of the data list that could contain the required data item. This is continued until there is only one item in the list you are examining.

This is the algorithm:

```
1.  found = False
2.  REPEAT
3.      Examine the middle data item in the list
4.      IF this is the required item THEN
5.          found = True
6.      ELSE
7.        IF required item > middle item THEN
8.            discard the first half of the list including middle item
9.        ELSE
10.           discard the second half of the list including middle item
11.       ENDIF
12.     ENDIF
13. UNTIL found = True OR there are no more items in the list
```

Example 4

Consider the following ordered list of 15 items. We want to find out whether the number 50 is in the list of 10 items.

15	21	29	32	37	40	42	43	48	50	60	64	77	81	90

Stage 1: The middle term is 43; we can therefore discard all data items less than or equal to 43.

48	50	60	64	77	81	90

Stage 2: The middle term is 64, so we can discard all data items greater than or equal to 64.

48	50	60

Stage 3: The middle term is **50** – so we have found the data item.

Note that if there are an even number of items in the list, for example eight items, then either the fourth (left) or fifth (right) item can be chosen as the middle item. For the following questions use the left item as the middle item if there is a choice.

Q19 Suppose we have the following sorted list of 10 items:

3	5	6	8	11	12	14	15	17	18

Which one of the following is the correct sequence of comparisons when used to locate the data item 8?

(i) 12, 6, 8   (ii) 11, 5, 6, 8   (iii) 3, 5, 6, 8   (iv) 11, 6, 5, 8

Q20 Ask a friend to think of a number between 1 and 1000. Then use a binary search algorithm to guess the number. How many different guesses will you need, at most?

Q21 Look at the following data list. Which items will you examine in (a) a linear search and (b) a binary search to find the following data items: 27, 11, 60?

9	11	19	22	27	30	32	33	40	42	50	54	57	61	70	78	85

Comparing linear and binary search algorithms

When comparing searches, consider their fitness for purpose and efficiency. Efficiency is usually considered by the number of comparisons, number of passes through a loop or the amount of memory that is used.

The linear search algorithm is fine for just a few items, but for a very large number of items, it is very inefficient. The average time taken to search 1000 items will be 100 times longer than the time taken to search 10 items. If you had to search a database of 10 million car registrations to find who owns a certain car, it would take a very long time.

In contrast, the binary search algorithm is extremely efficient. Each time an item is examined, if it is not the right one, half the list is discarded. In a list of 10 million items, only 24 items would need to be examined. That's because 10,000,000 is less than 2^{24}. In general, if there are fewer than 2^n items (but at least 2^{n-1}), the maximum number of items that needs to be examined is n.

A key benefit of the linear search is that it can be done on an unsorted list - the items do not have to be in sequence. If items are frequently added or deleted from the list, this saves the extra work needed to keep the list in sequence in order to do a binary search.

Q22 When searching for a number between 1 and 1000, compare the efficiency of using a linear search against that of a binary search.

1.5 – Sorting algorithms

In the last sub-section we looked at methods of searching for data. The binary search method required the data to be sorted before the search could take place. There are many algorithms for sorting data and we will look at two of them:

- Bubble sort
- Merge sort

Bubble sort

A bubble sort works by repeatedly going through the list to be sorted, comparing each pair of adjacent elements. If the elements are in the wrong order they are swapped. A short algorithm to do the swapping is:

```
temp = a
a = b
b = temp
```

If a = 9 and b = 6, the **trace table** below shows that the values of a and b have been swapped.

temp	a	b
	9	6
9	6	9

Q23 Explain the problem with writing the two statements below to swap the values.

a = b

b = a

Example 5: Working through the Bubble sort algorithm

The figure below shows how the items change order in the first pass, as the largest item 'bubbles' to the end of the list. Each time an item is larger than the next one, they change places.

Pass 1							
9	**5**	4	15	3	8	11	2
5	**9**	**4**	15	3	8	11	2
5	4	**9**	**15**	3	8	11	2
5	4	9	**15**	**3**	8	11	2
5	4	9	3	**15**	**8**	11	2
5	4	9	3	8	**15**	**11**	2
5	4	9	3	8	11	**15**	**2**
5	4	9	3	8	11	2	**15**

After the first pass as shown above, the largest item is in the correct place at the end of the list. On the second pass, only the first seven numbers are checked.

| End of pass 2 | 4 | 5 | 3 | 8 | 9 | 2 | 11 | 15 |

11 and 15 are in the correct place; so only the first 6 numbers are checked.

| End of pass 3 | 4 | 3 | 5 | 8 | 2 | 9 | 11 | 15 |

9, 11 and 15 are now in the correct place; so only the first 5 numbers are checked.

| End of pass 4 | 3 | 4 | 5 | 2 | 8 | 9 | 11 | 15 |

8, 9, 11 and 15 are now in the correct place; so only the first 4 numbers are checked.

| End of pass 5 | 3 | 4 | 2 | 5 | 8 | 9 | 11 | 15 |

5, 8, 9, 11 and 15 are now in the correct place; so only the first 3 numbers are checked.

| End of pass 6 | 3 | 2 | 4 | 5 | 8 | 9 | 11 | 15 |

Finally, the first two numbers are checked and swapped

| End of pass 7 | 2 | 3 | 4 | 5 | 8 | 9 | 11 | 15 |

The numbers are now in the correct order, and no further pass is required.

Algorithm for a bubble sort

In this algorithm, numbers is an array holding eight numbers. Each element of the array is referred to using an index in square brackets. In the array below, the first element of the array, 9, is held in numbers[0], and the last element, 2, is held in numbers[7].

Arrays are covered in **Section 6A.4**.

1

```
numbers = [9, 5, 4, 15, 3, 8, 11, 2]
numItems = len(numbers) #get number of items in the array
FOR i = 0 TO numItems - 2
  FOR j = 0 TO numItems - i - 2
    IF numbers[j] > numbers[j + 1] THEN
      temp = numbers[j]
      numbers[j] = numbers[j + 1]
      numbers[j + 1] = temp
    ENDIF
  ENDFOR
  OUTPUT numbers
ENDFOR
```

If you run this program, the output is:

```
[5, 4, 9, 3, 8, 11, 2, 15]
[4, 5, 3, 8, 9, 2, 11, 15]
[4, 3, 5, 8, 2, 9, 11, 15]
[3, 4, 5, 2, 8, 9, 11, 15]
[3, 4, 2, 5, 8, 9, 11, 15]
[3, 2, 4, 5, 8, 9, 11, 15]
[2, 3, 4, 5, 8, 9, 11, 15]
```

Using a flag

Sometimes, a flag is tested on each pass so that if no swaps are made during a pass through the items, no more unnecessary passes are made through an already sorted list.

Suppose the list of numbers to be sorted is [7, 2, 3, 4, 5, 8, 9, 11, 15].

A flag variable called, for example, swapMade is set to False at the beginning of each pass. On the first pass, when a swap is made, swapMade is changed from False to True.

After the first pass, the numbers will be in the sequence [2, 3, 4, 5, 7, 8, 9, 11, 15] and are already in sequence.

On the second pass, as no swaps are made, swapMade remains False. This condition is tested, the loop ends and no more passes are made.

Here is the amended algorithm:

```
numbers = [7, 2, 3, 4, 5, 8, 9, 11, 15]
numItems = len(numbers) #get number of items in the array
swapMade = True #indicates when a swap is made
i = 0
WHILE i < (numItems - 1) AND swapMade
  swapMade = False
  FOR j = 0 TO numItems - i - 2
    IF numbers[j] > numbers[j + 1] THEN
      temp = numbers[j]
      numbers[j] = numbers[j + 1]
      numbers[j + 1] = temp
      swapMade = True
    ENDIF
  ENDFOR
  i = i + 1
ENDWHILE
OUTPUT numbers
```

If a pass is completed without any swaps being made, the flag remains False and the WHILE loop ends. The sort is complete.

Q24 Carry out a bubble sort on the following set of numbers. The numbers should be sorted in DESCENDING ORDER (highest to lowest).

6	8	1	17	27	11	15	3	14	42	5

(a) What is the order of the items after the first pass?

(b) (i) Using the simple bubble sort method which does not use a flag, how many passes through the data will be made?

(ii) What is the maximum number of passes on a list of 2 items?

(iii) What is the maximum number of passes on a list of 3 items? 10,000 items?

Merge sort

This is a two stage sort. In the first stage, the list is successively divided in half, forming two sublists, until each sublist is of length one.

Example 6: Sorting a list in ascending order

Stage 1

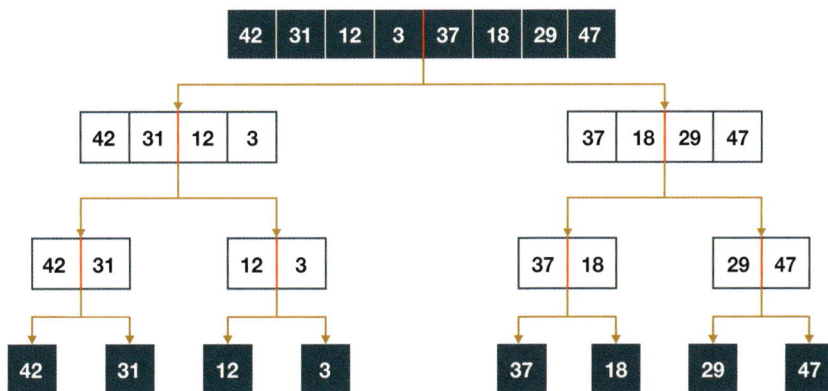

This is the end of stage 1 where all the elements have been separated out.

In the second stage, each pair of sublists is repeatedly merged to produce new sorted sublists until there is only one sublist remaining. As each pair of lists is merged, they are merged in order. Merging the final two sublists results in the sorted list.

Stage 2

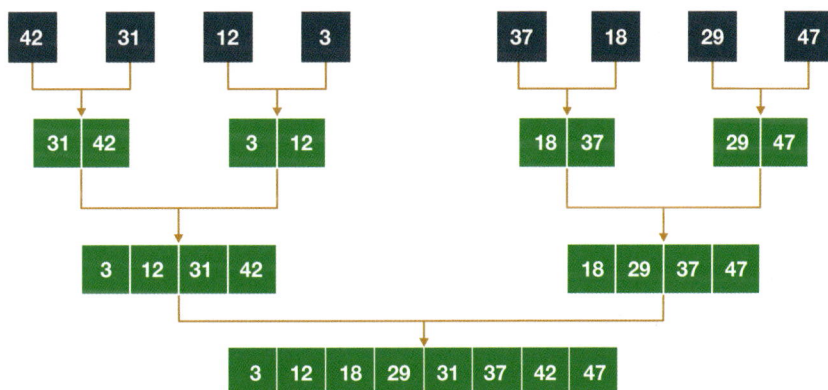

Q25 Carry out a merge sort on the following set of numbers. The numbers are to be sorted in ascending order.

6	8	1	17	27	11	15	3

(a) Write out the four sorted sublists after the first phase of Stage 2 (the merge process).

(b) Write out the two sorted sublists after the second phase of the merge process.

(c) Write out the complete list after the third phase of the merge process.

Q26 Which algorithm, the bubble sort or the merge sort, do you think is more efficient? Explain your choice.

Comparing the merge sort and bubble sort algorithms

The bubble sort algorithm is very slow and inefficient for sorting more than a very few items. We saw that in a list of just eight items, seven passes through the data had to be made. On each pass, it is likely that some items will need to be swapped. You can imagine how long it would take to sort a million items using a bubble sort! Roughly speaking, to sort n items will need n^2 comparisons.

The merge sort, rather like the binary search, works by successively halving the data set. In this algorithm, this operation is repeated until each sublist is only one item long. Then the sublists are recombined. This is a much more efficient process than the bubble sort as it takes much less time to execute.

The disadvantage for an inexperienced programmer is that it is a more difficult algorithm to implement. Another disadvantage is that it requires more memory to store the sublists, which can be a problem with a very large list. Merge sort is therefore less efficient in its use of memory than bubble sort.

Efficiency of algorithms

We have looked at two algorithms for searching a list, and two algorithms for sorting a list. In each case, either of the algorithms can be used to solve the problem, but one algorithm is much more efficient.

When performing a binary search, for example, doubling the size of the list from 1000 to 2000 items only involves halving the list one more time. Using a linear search, it could mean searching an extra thousand items!

Q27 Is a binary search always faster than a linear search? Explain your answer.

Many problems, both simple and complex, have more than one method of solution. Consider the problem of finding the sum of the integers from 1 to n. Here are two different algorithms for solving this problem.

Algorithm 1:

```
total = 0
FOR i = 1 TO n
  total = total + n
ENDFOR
```

Algorithm 2:

```
total = n *(n + 1)/2
```

The second algorithm is clearly much more efficient, as only one instruction is executed.

Q28 How many instructions are executed using each of the algorithms if n = 1000?

1.6 – Logic diagrams and truth tables

Binary logic in programming

Understanding how binary logic works will help your programming. In your programs you often use complex Boolean expressions to control loops and selection statements – for example:

```
while not(endOfFile) and not (itemFound) ......
if (x <= 10) or (currentCharNum > lengthOfString) ......
```

You may have created a program to repeat a section of code if the user presses "Y" or "y". The loop would look something like this:

```
WHILE (response == "Y") OR (response == "y")
```

Boolean Expression   *Boolean Expression*

Each Boolean expression can be replaced with a letter which is called a Boolean variable.

```
WHILE (response == "Y") OR (response == "y")
```

Replace with the   *Replace with the*
Boolean variable, X   *Boolean variable, Y*

```
WHILE      X          OR          Y
```

1

Just like the Boolean data type in programming, Boolean variables are either **True** or **False**. X and Y will be either True or False. We equate True with 1 and False with 0 to represent electronic circuits being open or closed, just like with binary.

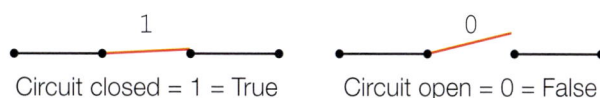

1   0

Circuit closed = 1 = True   Circuit open = 0 = False

Logic diagrams

Computers are based on electrical circuits where we can detect whether current is flowing or not. Binary uses base 2, so we have just two possible values, 1 or 0. Representing data as binary values means we have to detect just two values in electrical circuits.

Binary logic uses these most basic circuits. Circuits in computers are made up of many logic gates but at this level we are looking at just three of them: NOT, AND and OR. A given input will generate an output based on the logic gate in use.

We use specific symbols to represent the different logic gates; these are standard symbols. They can be used to represent Boolean expressions such as Q = NOT A AND (B OR C).

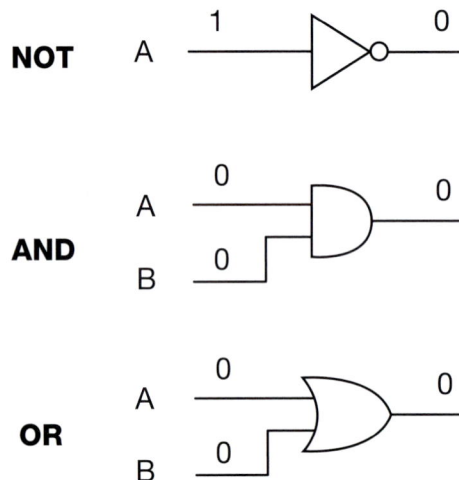

The logic gates can be joined up to make a circuit. For example P = NOT (A OR (B AND C)):

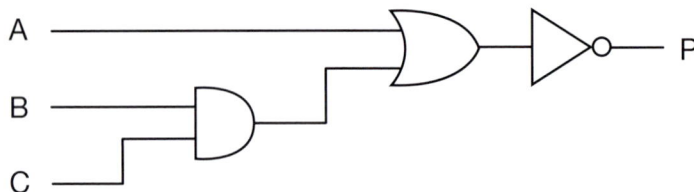

Logic gates and truth tables

Each of the NOT, AND and OR gates can be represented by a truth table showing the output, given each possible input or combination of inputs. Inputs are usually given algebraic letters such as A, B and C and output is usually represented by P or Q.

NOT gate

The NOT gate is represented by the symbol below and inverts the input. The small circle denotes an inverted input. If A is 1 (True), then NOT A is 0 (False).

Using 1s and 0s as inputs to a gate, its operation can be summarised in the form of a **truth table**.

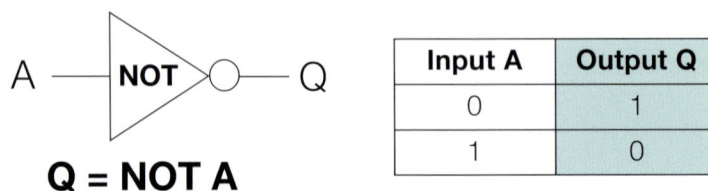

Q = NOT A

Input A	Output Q
0	1
1	0

AND gate

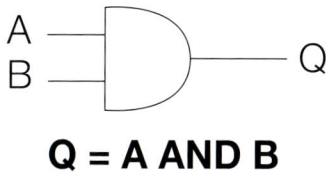

Q = A AND B

Input A	Input B	Output Q
0	0	0
0	1	0
1	0	0
1	1	1

The Boolean expression for AND is written: Q = A AND B.

The truth table reflects the fundamental property of the AND gate: the output of A AND B is 1 (True) only if input A and input B are both 1 (True).

OR gate

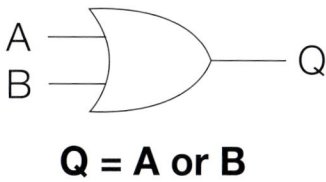

Q = A or B

Input A	Input B	Output Q
0	0	0
0	1	1
1	0	1
1	1	1

If A = 0 (False) and B = 0 (False) then A OR B = 0 (False), otherwise A OR B = 1 (True).

Combining logic gates into logic circuits

These logic gates can be combined to form more complex logic circuits which can carry out a number of functions. They are the basic building blocks of many electronic circuits found in computer memories, household devices, computer management systems in cars, and so on. Look at the logic circuit below and follow the accompanying truth table.

Example 1

The logic circuit below represents the Boolean condition P = (NOT A AND B) OR (A AND C).

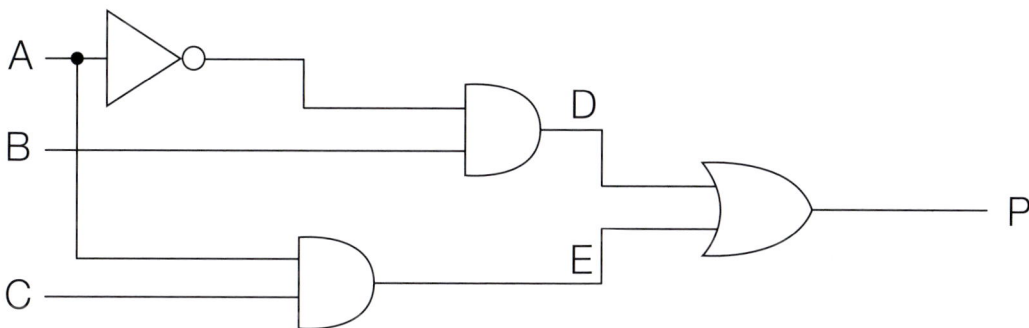

1

The truth table representing the logic circuit on the previous page:

A	B	C	NOT A	NOT A AND B	A AND C	(NOT A AND B) or (A AND C)
0	0	0	1	0	0	0
0	0	1	1	0	0	0
0	1	0	1	1	0	1
0	1	1	1	1	0	1
1	0	0	0	0	0	0
1	0	1	0	0	1	1
1	1	0	0	0	0	0
1	1	1	0	0	1	1

Q29 Write the expression representing the logic circuit below, and complete the truth table.

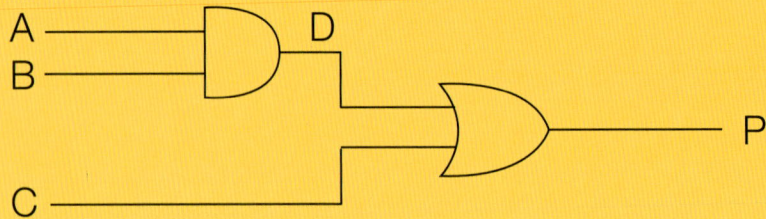

A	B	C	D = A and B	P = (A and B) or C
0	0	0		
0	0	1		
0	1	0		
0	1	1		
1	0	0		
1	0	1		
1	1	0		
1	1	1		

Exercises

1. **Abstraction** and **decomposition** are two aspects of computational thinking.

   (a) Sienna is designing a program to control a cat-flap which will open only when a cat belonging to its owner approaches.

   Describe **two** ways in which she may use abstraction in reaching a solution to this problem. [2]

   (b) A program is required to enter a set of students' examination marks, count the number of students who obtained each mark and output the counts for each mark. Examination marks entered must be in the range 0 to 100.

   Explain how **decomposition** might be used in designing a solution to this problem. [3]

2. (a) (i) A bubble sort is used to sort the following numbers in ascending order:

   34, 56, 89, 23, 12, 77, 49, 44

   Write the order that the numbers will be in after the first pass. [2]

   (ii) State the number of passes required to sort the items. (No flag is used to indicate a sorted list.) [1]

   (b) A **merge sort** is to be used to sort the same numbers. During the merge phase, the following four pairs of numbers need to be merged into two groups of four.

   (34, 56), (23, 89), (12, 77), (44, 49)

   Write the contents of each group of four numbers after the next phase of the merge. [2]

   1

3. A list of surnames is held in sorted order. The names are:

   Beck, Coe, Ford, Grey, Hill, Kerr, Lunn, Pugh, Ross, Shaw, Taft, Ward

   (a) State which names would be examined when searching for the name **Grey** using:

   (i) a linear search [1]

   (ii) a binary search [1]

   (b) State which names would be examined when searching for the name **James** using:

   (i) a linear search [1]

   (ii) a binary search [1]

   (c) In a list of 1000 items, state the maximum number of names that would have to be searched to find a particular name using:

   (i) a linear search [1]

   (ii) a binary search [1]

4.   A school uses a computer program to give every new pupil a username for logging onto computers. The algorithm used to choose the username is shown below.

(a)   Emily Smith joins the school in 2024. No other pupil called Smith joins the school in the same year.

State the username which Emily will be given and explain how you obtained your answer from the flowchart.   [3]

(b)   A pupil has the username 2023gillc##.

State **four** facts that you can work out from this username.   [4]

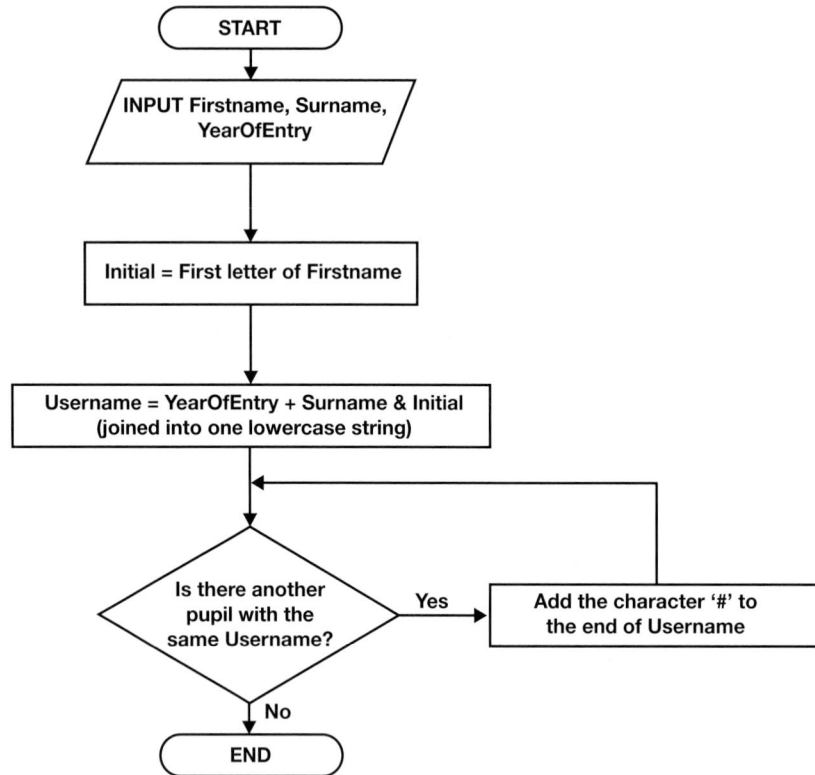

5.   A café sells three types of item:

iced bun	£1.50
cup cake	£2.00
muffin	£1.20

Write an algorithm using either a flowchart or pseudocode which:

- inputs every item sold during the day
- adds up the total amount taken for each item
- outputs the total takings for each item
- outputs the type of item that had the highest takings at the end of the day.   [6]

6. Look at the flowchart below.

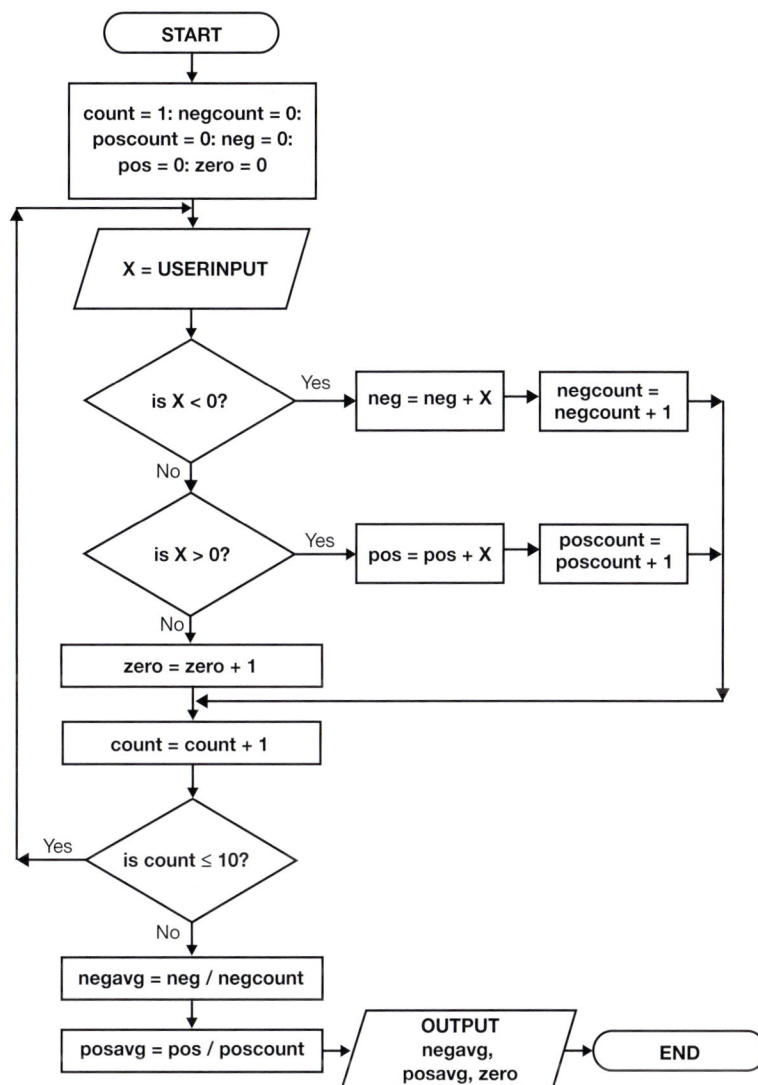

(a) Complete the trace table using the input data supplied and the headings given. [7]

Input data: 0, 8, 7, 10, -8, -7, 0, 0, -3, 11

X	neg	negcount	pos	poscount	zero	count	count ≤ 10?	negavg	posavg	Output

(b) Give the purpose of this algorithm. [3]

7. (a) State the output of each of the following logic gates for the inputs given. [3]

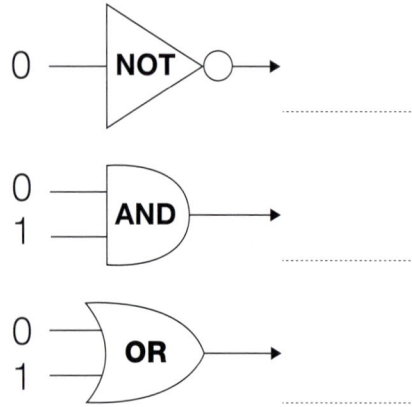

0 — NOT ....

0
1 AND ....

0
1 OR ....

(b) Figure 1 is a circuit diagram.

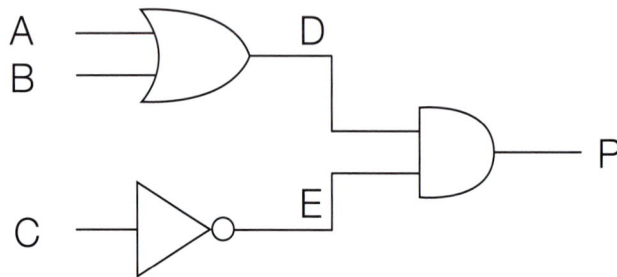

A
B → D

C → E

P

Figure 1

Complete the truth table for Figure 1. [3]

A	B	C	D = A OR B	E = NOT C	P = D AND E
0	0	0			
0	0	1			
0	1				
0	1				
1					
1					
1					
1					

Section 2

Data

Objectives

- Understand that computers use binary to represent numbers, text, sound, graphics and program instructions
- Be able to determine the maximum number of states that can be represented by a binary pattern of a given length
- Be able to represent unsigned integers using binary (0 to 255)
- Be able to represent negative numbers using two's complement signed integers (-128 to +127)
- Convert between denary and 8-bit binary numbers
- Be able to add two positive binary patterns
- Apply logical and arithmetic binary shifts
- Understand the concept of overflow
- Understand why hexadecimal notation is used
- Convert between hexadecimal and binary
- Understand how computers encode characters using 7-bit ASCII
- Know how bitmap images are represented in binary including the concepts of pixels, resolution and colour depth
- Know how analogue sound is represented in binary including the concepts of amplitude, sample rate, bit depth and sample interval
- Understand the limitations of binary representation of data when constrained by the number of available bits
- Understand the data storage units bit, nibble, byte, kibibyte, mebibyte, gibibyte and tebibyte
- Be able to construct expressions to calculate file sizes and data capacity requirements
- Understand the need for data compression and both lossy and lossless compression methods

2

2.1 – Storage units and binary numbers

Computers are made up of complicated hardware that stores and processes data. If you break a computer down into its most basic components you have millions of circuits that either allow electricity to flow, or not. Imagine a whole row of light switches that you can switch on and off in different combinations to mean different things. Each switch is either on or off. It has only two states, which can be represented by 1 or 0. This is called **binary**.

All data, such as numbers, program instructions, text, sound and graphics are stored and processed as binary.

A single **1** or **0** is a **bi**nary digi**t**, or a **bit** for short. A group of eight bits is called a **byte**. Imagine you've taken a small bite out of an apple, you might call that a nibble. So four bits, half a byte, is called a **nibble**.

Units

A byte is the smallest addressable unit of memory in a computer. Just as a kilometre is 1000 metres, we can group together 1000 bytes to make a **kilobyte**. In Computer Science, memory is often considered using powers of 2. So, a **kibibyte** is 2^{10} = 1,024 bytes, a **mebibyte** is 2^{20} = 1,048,576 bytes, and so on.

Memory size is measured in the following multiples:

Unit	Number of bytes	Number of bytes	Equivalent to
Kibibyte (kiB)	2^{10}	1,024 bytes	1,024 bytes
Mebibyte (MiB)	2^{20}	1,048,576 bytes	1,024 kiB
Gibibyte (GiB)	2^{30}	1,073,741,824 bytes	1,024 MiB
Tebibyte (TiB)	2^{40}	1,099,511,627,776 bytes	1,024 GiB

(**Note:** An alternative system of units makes use of standard prefixes, with 1 kilobyte = 1000 bytes, 1 megabyte = 1,000,000 bytes, 1 gigabyte = 1,000,000,000 bytes, 1 terabyte = 1,000,000,000,000 bytes.)

Q1
(a) Convert 2,048 MiB into GiB
(b) Convert 1 TiB into GiB

Q2
(a) How much storage is needed for a typical photograph file taken from a mobile phone camera?
(b) A music streaming service has 1 million tracks. A typical track requires 3 MiB. How much storage will be needed to store all the tracks?

Computers use the binary system to store numbers and perform binary arithmetic and logic operations. The storage capacities of computer systems have grown, and the memory size of secondary storage systems is now commonly measured in tebibytes (TiB).

Binary

Binary data uses only two digits, 0 and 1. Our denary system uses ten digits, 0 to 9. The number 75, for example, is 7 tens plus 5 units.

Imagine you are back in primary school, learning to add again. 7 + 5 = 12, so you write down the 2 units but carry the group of 10. 23 would be 2 groups of 10 and 3 units.

Counting in binary

Counting in binary is the same except instead of digits 0 to 9 we only have two digits, 0 and 1, so we carry the group of 2. This is known as base 2 or binary. This is how we count to ten in binary:

Denary	Binary	
0	0	
1	1	
2	10	Notice that 1 + 1 = 10 in binary, just as in denary, 9 + 1 = 10
3	11	One group of 2 plus one unit 2 + 1 = 3
4	100	Notice that 11 + 1 = 100 in binary, just as in denary, 99 + 1 = 100
5	101	
6	110	
7	111	
8	1000	
9	1001	
10	1010	

Look at the pattern of the column headings. Notice how for binary numbers they double each time.

128	64	32	16	8	4	2	1
2x2x2x2x2x2x2	2x2x2x2x2x2	2x2x2x2x2	2x2x2x2	2x2x2	2x2	2	1
2^7	2^6	2^5	2^4	2^3	2^2	2^1	2^0

Q3 Looking at the table above, what is 2^8?

Storing larger numbers

In order to store larger numbers, computers group 2, 4, 8 or more bytes into units called **words**. On this course you will be dealing only with binary numbers held in a single 8-bit byte.

Number of states

A binary pattern of a given length is able to store a maximum number of states. For example, a 1 digit binary number can represent two states (0, 1) and a 2 digit binary number can represent four states (00, 01, 10, 11).

$$\text{maximum number of states} = 2^{(\text{binary number length})}$$

So, for example, the maximum number of states an 8 bit number can represent is $2^8 = 256$ (often used to represent the numbers of 0~255). The maximum number of states a 16-bit number can represent is $2^{16} = 65,536$.

Q4 What is the maximum number of states that a four bit number can represent?

Denary to binary conversion

To convert a denary number to a binary number, use the tables below. You need to find the highest number in the column heading that you can take away from the number and start there:

To convert the denary number **57** into binary:

The highest column heading we can take out of 57 is 32 (the next one is 64, which is too high).

We can start by placing a "1" in the column headed 32 (57-32=25)

we can then place a "1" in the column headed 16 (25-16=9)

Finally place "1"s in columns 8 and 1 (9-8=1)

128	64	32	16	8	4	2	1
0	0	1	1	1	0	0	1

Here are some more examples:

Denary	Binary							
	128	64	32	16	8	4	2	1
23	0	0	0	1	0	1	1	1
84	0	1	0	1	0	1	0	0
255	1	1	1	1	1	1	1	1

Each binary digit is called a **bit**. A group of eight bits is called a **byte**. You will notice in the examples above that we always write the binary numbers using eight bits. This is common practice. It is not incorrect to write the first binary value as 1 0 1 1 1 rather than 0 0 0 1 0 1 1 1 (without the leading zeros) but the second example is more commonly used.

Q5 Convert the following denary numbers into binary.
(a) 19   (b) 63   (c) 142

Binary to denary conversion

To convert a binary number into denary, we add up the column values where a "1" appears. For example, to convert the binary number 01101100 to denary, write each number under a column heading, starting on the right with the least significant bit:

128	64	32	16	8	4	2	1
0	1	1	0	1	1	0	0

gives the value: **64** + **32** + **8** + **4** = **108**

More examples:

Denary	Binary							
	128	64	32	16	8	4	2	1
126	0	1	1	1	1	1	1	0
213	1	1	0	1	0	1	0	1
254	1	1	1	1	1	1	1	0

Q6 Convert the following binary numbers into denary.
(a) 00010111   (b) 10010110   (c) 11111111

2.2 – Binary arithmetic and hexadecimal

Addition of binary numbers

Adding binary works in exactly the same way as adding denary numbers except this time you carry groups of 2 instead of groups of 10:

Adding in denary	Adding in binary
1 2 3 4 5	1 0 0 1 0
1 3 4 +	1 0 1 +
1 2 4 7 9	1 0 1 1 1
7 8 2 3 5	1 0 0 1 1
$_1$9$_1$7 +	$_1$1$_1$1$_1$1 +
7 8 3 3 2	1 1 0 1 0

Notice that you carry 1 when you get to ten in a column so 5+7=12, write 2 in that column but carry 1 group of ten.

Notice that:
0 + 0 = 0
0 + 1 or 1 + 0 = 1
1 + 1 = 0 carry 1
1 + 1 + 1 = 1 carry 1

Some more examples:

```
  10101100      00101101      00101101
  00010001+     10000101+     10000111+
  10111101      10110010      10110100
```

> **Q7** Carry out the following binary number additions:
> (a) 00110011 + 01000110
> (b) 00010110 + 01110110
> (c) 00001111 + 01110011
> (d) 00101010 + 01111011
> (e) 00011100 + 01110011

Overflow

The biggest number you can represent with 8 bits is 255 (i.e. 128+64+32+16+8+4+2+1).

If you add two binary numbers together that result in a number bigger than 255, it will need 9 or more bits. A computer stores items in memory in a finite amount of space. If you cannot represent the number in that amount of space because it is too big, then **overflow** occurs.

For example:

```
(252)  11111100
 (15)  00001111+
(267) 100001011
```

The computer would need 9 bits to represent 267 so this 9th bit doesn't fit in the byte allocated. This will cause an **overflow** error.

Hexadecimal number system

Which of these is easier to remember: 01011011 or 5B? Humans are not very good at remembering long strings of numbers so, to make it easier, we can represent every group of 4 bits (known as a **nibble**) with a single digit.

The smallest value you can hold in 4 bits is 0000. The largest value is 1111. This means that we need to represent the denary values 0 to 15 with a single digit. The trouble is, we only have numerical digits 0 to 9, so to get around this problem we use letters A to F to represent the digits 10, 11, 12, 13, 14 and 15.

This is called base 16 or, more commonly, **hexadecimal**. It is often abbreviated to **hex**.

Denary	Binary	Hex
0	0000	0
1	0001	1
2	0010	2
3	0011	3
4	0100	4
5	0101	5
6	0110	6
7	0111	7
8	1000	8
9	1001	9
10	1010	A
11	1011	B
12	1100	C
13	1101	D
14	1110	E
15	1111	F
16	0001 0000	10
255	1111 1111	FF

A single hex digit replaces 4 bits. 15 is the biggest number you can have with 4 bits so 16 is one group of 16 and no units (just like we did with binary)

255 represents 15 groups of 16 + 15 units = (15 x 16) + 15 = 240 + 15

Converting a binary number to hexadecimal

In GCSE Computer Science you will only need to work with 8-bit binary numbers, which can be represented as two hex digits. The left-hand hex digit represents groups of 16, the right-hand hex digit represents the units.

The denary number 92 =   **0101**   **1100**   = **5C** in hex
                          5   **12**   *(12 is replaced by C – see table above)*

Q8 Convert the following numbers from binary to hex:

(a) 00010111

(b) 11111100

(c) 001100101110

(d) 1101110001111111

Converting a denary number to hexadecimal

To convert the denary number 182 into hex the first step is to work out how many groups of 16 there are in 182. Secondly work out how many units are left over.

182 / 16 = 11 remainder 6

11 is B in hex. 6 is just 6   so 182 denary = B6 hex

Alternatively, you can convert the denary to binary first and then convert the binary to hex.

> **Q9** Convert the following numbers from denary to hex:
> (a) 77   (b) 255   (c) 186   (d) 18

Converting hexadecimal to binary

Converting a hexadecimal number into binary is a simple matter of converting each hex digit into a group of 4 binary digits. For example, to convert the hex number **A7** to binary:

A   **7**

1010   **0111**

Further examples: **B5** is 1 0 1 1   0 1 0 1
                      FA is 1 1 1 1   1 0 1 0

> **Q10** Convert the following hexadecimal numbers into binary:
> (a) E4   (b) 8A   (c) FF   (d) C1

Converting hexadecimal to denary

To convert a hexadecimal number into denary, multiply the heading values by the hex digit. For example, to convert the hex number **A7** to denary:

A   **7**   (remember column place values are: **16** and **1**)

(10 x 16)   +   **(7 x 1)**   = **167** (remember: A = 10)

Further examples: **7F** is 112 + 15 = **127**
                      CD is 192 + 13 = **205**

> **Q11** Convert the following hexadecimal numbers into denary:
> (a) 77   (b) AF   (c) 17   (d) 20

Uses of hexadecimal

As hexadecimal is so much easier for humans to understand and remember than binary, it has several applications in computing. One application you are probably familiar with is picking colours for a graphic.

Hex numbers are also used in assembly language instructions such as `ADD &4F3A`.

2

2.3 – Two's complement and binary shifts

Two's complement

Previously you have looked at binary to denary conversions that use positive integers. These are known as **unsigned** integers as there is no + or – sign at the start of the number.

When storing numbers, only binary 1s and 0s can be used. A system known as two's complement is used to store both negative and positive numbers using one bit pattern.

Imagine an analogue counter. As you turn it back, it goes from 0001 to 0000 to 9999.

0001 *Turn back* **0000** *Turn back* **9999**

The 9999 then represents the number -1. 9998 would represent -2.

Two's complement numbers work in the same way using binary numbers.

Two's complement	Denary
1000 0000	-128
1000 0001	-127
...	
1111 1110	-2
1111 1111	-1
0000 0000	0
0000 0001	1
0000 0010	2
...	
0111 1101	125
0111 1110	126
0111 1111	127

Q12 Give the 8-bit two's complement binary that represents the number +3.
Use the table above to help you.

Q13 Give the 8-bit two's complement binary that represents the number -3.
Use the table above to help you.

Converting a denary number to two's complement binary

Converting positive denary numbers to two's complement is exactly the same as unsigned binary number conversions. For example:

Positive denary number	Unsigned binary number	Two's complement
1	0000 0001	0000 0001
5	0000 0101	0000 0101
17	0001 0001	0001 0001

Converting a negative denary number to two's complement is a little harder.
Use the following steps:

1 Convert the positive of the denary number to binary.

2 Flip all the bits (0 to 1 and 1 to 0).

3 Add 1.

For example, to convert -18 to its two's complement equivalent:

1 18 in binary is 0001 0010.

2 Flip all the bits: 1110 1101.

3 Add 1: 1110 1110.
   The two's complement of -18 is therefore: 1110 1110.

Converting a two's complement binary number to a denary number

When a two's complement binary number starts with a 1 it represents a negative number.

To convert this to a denary number, the same method as above is used in reverse:

1 Subtract 1.

2 Flip all the bits.

3 Convert the number to denary and add a minus symbol at the start.

To convert the two's complement number 1010 1011 to denary:

1 Subtract 1: 1010 1010.

2 Flip all the bits: 01010101.

3 Convert the number to denary: =64+16+4+1 = 85

Add a minus at the start: -85

The denary of the two's complement number 1010 1011 is therefore -85.

> **Q14** Convert the denary number -57 to two's complement.

> **Q15** Convert the two's complement number 1011 0110 to denary.

2

Binary shifts

Binary shifts involve moving the digits of binary numbers to the left or right. There are two types of binary shift – **logical shift** and **arithmetic shift**.

Logical shifts

If a binary number is shifted to the left this is equivalent to multiplying the number by 2 for each shift to the left. For example: If we shift

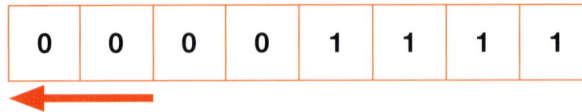

0	0	0	0	1	1	1	1

⟵

TWO places to the left we get the binary number:

0	0	1	1	1	1	0	0

(NOTE: Empty binary positions are filled with 0s as we shift to the left.)

The original binary number has a value of 15 (i.e. 1+2+4+8 = 15); the number after shifting two places to the left has the value 60 (i.e. 32+16+8+4 = 60). It is multiplied by 4, or 2^2. Note that shifting more than four places to the left in this example would result in an overflow error.

Shifting binary numbers to the right has the opposite effect i.e. each shift to the right has the effect of dividing by 2. Thus if we shift

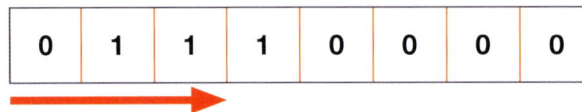

0	1	1	1	0	0	0	0

⟶

THREE places to the right we get the binary number:

0	0	0	0	1	1	1	0

The original binary value was 112 (i.e. 16+32+64 = 112) and the value after shifting three places to the right is 14 (i.e. 2+4+8 = 14). The number was divided by 8, or 2^3.

(NOTE: Empty binary positions are filled with 0s as we shift to the right.)

Multiplication/division by powers of 2

This gives an easy way to multiply and divide binary numbers by powers of 2.

- Shifting right one place divides the number by 2
- Shifting left one place multiplies the number by 2

Note that performing a logical left shift of two places on the 8-bit binary number 01000000 would give 00000000, causing **overflow**. In practice, multiplication is usually done differently and you need not be concerned with this issue.

> **Q16** Write down the results after the following shift operations and write down the denary values before and after the shifts:
>
> (a) The number 11001100 is shifted TWO places to the right
>
> (b) The number 00011001 is shifted TWO places to the left
>
> (c) The number 11001000 is shifted THREE places to the right
>
> (d) The number 00000111 is shifted FOUR places to the left
>
> (e) The number 10000000 is shifted FIVE places to the right

Arithmetic shifts

If a **logical shift** is used with a negative number stored in two's complement there is an issue.

For example, if we shift the number 1111 1110 (-2) one place to the right using a logical shift the result is 0111 1111 (127).

Instead, an arithmetic shift can be used. In a **right arithmetic shift** all the bits are moved right, but the left-most (sign) bit is replicated.

For example, if we shift

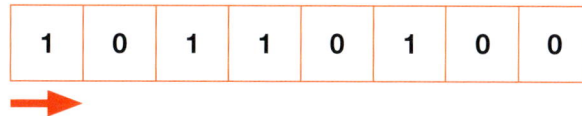

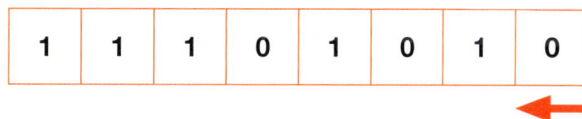

1	0	1	1	0	1	0	0

ONE place to the right we get the binary number:

1	1	0	1	1	0	1	0

Notice that the left-most bit still remains as 1.

In two's complement, the first binary number is -76 whilst the second binary number after the right arithmetic shift is -38.

The first number has been successfully divided by 2 and the negative sign has been kept.

A **left arithmetic shift** works in the same way as a logical shift. All the bits are moved left and a zero is added to the right hand side.

For example, if we shift

1	1	1	0	1	0	1	0

ONE place to the left we get the binary number:

1	1	0	1	0	1	0	0

Notice that the right-most bit has been filled with a 0.

In two's complement the first binary number is -22 whilst the second binary number after the left arithmetic shift is -44.

The first number has been successfully multiplied by 2 and the negative sign has been kept.

Q17 Write down the results after the following **arithmetic** shift operations and write down the denary values before and after the shifts. Note that the numbers are all in two's complement.

(a) The number 00010101 is shifted ONE place to the left
(b) The number 00110100 is shifted ONE place to the right
(c) The number 11011010 is shifted ONE place to the right
(d) The number 11110100 is shifted ONE place to the right

2.4 – ASCII

Every time a character is typed on a keyboard a code number is transmitted to the computer. The code numbers are stored in binary. PCs sometimes use a **character set** called **ASCII**, American Standard Code for Information Interchange.

The table below shows a version of ASCII that uses 7 bits to code each character. The biggest number that can be held in seven bits is 1111111 in binary (127 in denary). Therefore 128 different characters can be represented in the ASCII character set (using codes 0 to 127).

7-bit ASCII Table

ASCII	DEC	Binary	ASCII	DEC	Binary	ASCII	DEC	Binary	ASCII	DEC	Binary
NULL	000	000 0000	space	032	010 0000	@	064	100 0000	`	096	110 0000
SOH	001	000 0001	!	033	010 0001	A	065	100 0001	a	097	110 0001
STX	002	000 0010	"	034	010 0010	B	066	100 0010	b	098	110 0010
ETX	003	000 0011	#	035	010 0011	C	067	100 0011	c	099	110 0011
EOT	004	000 0100	$	036	010 0100	D	068	100 0100	d	100	110 0100
ENQ	005	000 0101	%	037	010 0101	E	069	100 0101	e	101	110 0101
ACK	006	000 0110	&	038	010 0110	F	070	100 0110	f	102	110 0110
BEL	007	000 0111	'	039	010 0111	G	071	100 0111	g	103	110 0111
BS	008	000 1000	(	040	010 1000	H	072	100 1000	h	104	110 1000
HT	009	000 1001	)	041	010 1001	I	073	100 1001	i	105	110 1001
LF	010	000 1010	*	042	010 1010	J	074	100 1010	j	106	110 1010
VT	011	000 1011	+	043	010 1011	K	075	100 1011	k	107	110 1011
FF	012	000 1100	,	044	010 1100	L	076	100 1100	l	108	110 1100
CR	013	000 1101	-	045	010 1101	M	077	100 1101	m	109	110 1101
SO	014	000 1110	.	046	010 1110	N	078	100 1110	n	110	110 1110
SI	015	000 1111	/	047	010 1111	O	079	100 1111	o	111	110 1111
DLE	016	001 0000	0	048	011 0000	P	080	101 0000	p	112	111 0000
DC1	017	001 0001	1	049	011 0001	Q	081	101 0001	q	113	111 0001
DC2	018	001 0010	2	050	011 0010	R	082	101 0010	r	114	111 0010
DC3	019	001 0011	3	051	011 0011	S	083	101 0011	s	115	111 0011
DC4	020	001 0100	4	052	011 0100	T	084	101 0100	t	116	111 0100
NAK	021	001 0101	5	053	011 0101	U	085	101 0101	u	117	111 0101
SYN	022	001 0110	6	054	011 0110	V	086	101 0110	v	118	111 0110
ETB	023	001 0111	7	055	011 0111	W	087	101 0111	w	119	111 0111
CAN	024	001 1000	8	056	011 1000	X	088	101 1000	x	120	111 1000
EM	025	001 1001	9	057	011 1001	Y	089	101 1001	y	121	111 1001
SUB	026	001 1010	:	058	011 1010	Z	090	101 1010	z	122	111 1010
ESC	027	001 1011	;	059	011 1011	[	091	101 1011	{	123	111 1011
FS	028	001 1100	<	060	011 1100	\	092	101 1100			124	111 1100
GS	029	001 1101	=	061	011 1101	]	093	101 1101	}	125	111 1101
RS	030	001 1110	>	062	011 1110	^	094	101 1110	~	126	111 1110
US	031	001 1111	?	063	011 1111	_	095	101 1111	DEL	127	111 1111

Using the ASCII table in programming

The character codes are grouped and run in sequence; i.e. if 'A' is 65 then 'C' must be 67. The pattern applies to other groupings such as digits and lowercase letters, so you can say that since '7' is 55, '9' must be 57.

Also, '7' < '9' and 'a' > 'A'.

Notice that the ASCII code value for '5' (0011 0101) is different from the pure binary value for 5 (0000 0101). That's why you can't perform calculations with user input. The input must first be converted to an integer.

2.5 – Images

Images can be stored in different ways on a computer. A drawing that you create in PowerPoint is a **vector** graphic. It is made up of lines and shapes with specific properties such as line style, line colour, fill colour, start point and end point. The computer stores all of this data about each shape in binary.

When you take a photograph on a digital camera, the image is not made up of individual shapes. The camera has to capture the continuously changing set of colours and shades that make up the real-life view. To store this type of image on a computer, the image is broken down into very small elements called **pixels**.

The **size** of an image is expressed directly as the width in pixels by height in pixels, e.g. 600 x 400. The **resolution** of an image is generally measured in **Pixels Per Inch** or **PPI**.

If the size of a picture is increased, then more pixels will need to be stored in order to maintain the same clarity or resolution. This increases the size of the image file. This is a **bitmap** image.

Colour depth

The image of a flower below uses four colours. Therefore two bits are needed to record the colour of each pixel.

The number of bits used to store each pixel dictates how many colours an image can contain. 8 bits per pixel will give 256 possible colours. The number of bits per pixel is referred to as the **colour depth**. To work out the minimum required colour depth from the number of colours in the image, convert the number of colours to a power of 2.

For up to:

2 = 2^1 colours	1 bit is required per pixel
4 = 2^2 colours	2 bits are required
8 = 2^3 colours	3 bits are required
...	
256 = 2^8 colours	8 bits are required
65,536 = 2^{16} colours	16 bits are required

If the **colour depth** is increased so more bits are used to represent each pixel, then the overall size of the file will increase.

If we record the value of each pixel in this image, starting from the top left-hand corner and going left to right across each row, we end up with the following data file:

        10 10 10 10 10 10 10 10

        10 00 10 00 10 00 10 10

        10 10 00 00 00 10 10 10

        10 00 00 01 00 00 10 10

    etc.

Q19 Convert the following binary data into a 5 x 5 pixel image, where 1 represents black and 0 represents white:

1 1 1 1 1   0 0 1 0 0   0 0 1 0 0   0 0 1 0 0   0 0 1 0 0

Q20 Convert the black and white image below into binary data, where 1 represents black and 0 represents white.

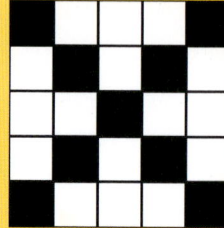

The effect of colour depth and resolution

Colour depth is used to describe the maximum number of colours that can be used to represent an image. The higher the number of colours, the more faithful the image will be. This will clearly also affect the file size of the image.

An image can be monochrome (black and white), grey scale (usually 256 shades of grey), 16-bit colour and 24-bit colour (known as true colour), for example.

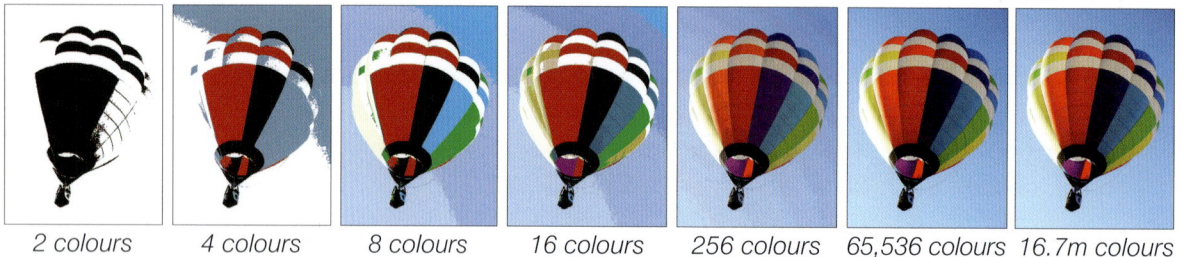

| 2 colours | 4 colours | 8 colours | 16 colours | 256 colours | 65,536 colours | 16.7m colours |

In true colour, there are 24 bits available for each pixel. 8 bits are used to represent each of the red channel, green channel and blue channel (RGB) of the pixel. Hence 24 bits are required for the whole pixel.

The **resolution** of an image is the number of pixels (picture elements) or dots that make up an image. The greater the number of pixels, the sharper the image will be, and the larger the file size of the image. Pixel density, measured in pixels per inch (PPI), is used to describe the resolution of a computer screen, camera or scanner.

An image from the internet is typically 72PPI, which is a low resolution. If you try to enlarge the image on the screen, the software makes up for the pixels which don't exist and you get a blurred image. The higher the resolution, the larger the image you can display on a screen without it looking blurred.

The resolution of a printed image is measured in dots per inch (DPI) rather than pixels per inch (PPI). If the dots on a printed page or pixels on a screen are smaller then the picture becomes clearer. At resolutions above 300 DPI the human eye is unlikely to detect the individual dots in a printed document.

Example 1 Calculating the file size

An image captured in 256 colours, with a size of 2,100 pixels by 1,500 pixels, is saved on a memory stick. What is the size in bytes of the file?

Size in bytes = (image width x image height x colour depth) / 8

= (2,100 x 1,500 x 8) / 8 (256 colours = colour depth of 8 bits)

= 3,150,000 bytes

Q21 Calculate the size in bytes of a black and white image that is 96 pixels wide and 1,024 pixels high.

2.6 – Sound

Sound waves are **analogue**, which means continuously changing. The height of the wave is known as the **amplitude**. Anything stored on a computer has to be stored in a **digital** format as a series of binary numbers. To store sound on a computer we need to convert the waveform into a numerical representation. The device that takes real-world analogue signals and converts them to a digital representation is called an **Analogue-to-Digital Converter** (**ADC**).

For sound waves, the analogue signal is converted as follows:

- Analogue sound is received by a microphone
- This is converted into an electrical analogue signal
- The signal amplitude (height of the wave) is measured at regular intervals (sampled)
- The values are rounded to a level (quantisation)
- The values are stored as a series of binary numbers

A **sample** is a measure of amplitude at a point in time. The accuracy with which an analogue sound wave is converted to a digital format depends on two things, **bit depth** and **sample rate**.

The bit depth is the number of bits used to store each sample. The two graphs below show how the amplitude of a wave is more accurately represented with a 4-bit depth than a 2-bit one.

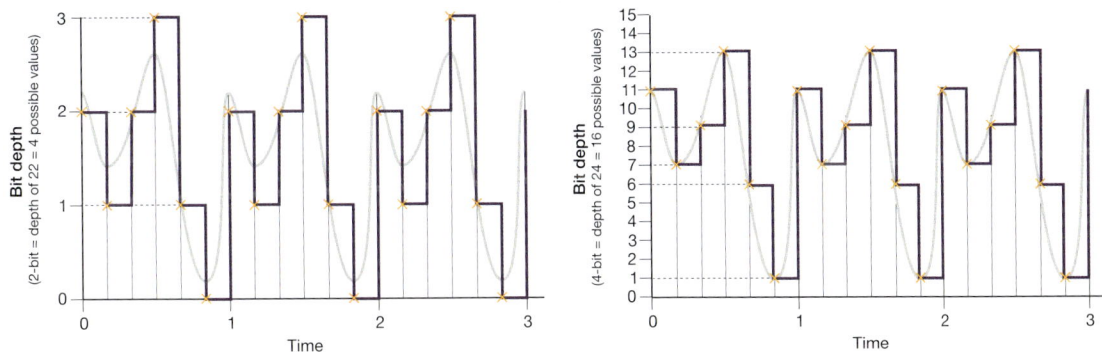

The **sample rate** is the frequency with which you record the amplitude of the sound, i.e. the number of samples per second. This is usually measured in **hertz**, where 1 hertz = 1 sample per second. The more frequently the sound is sampled, the better the quality of playback.

The more often you take a sample, the smoother the playback will sound. The two graphs below show how changing the sample rate increases or decreases the accuracy of the digital representation.

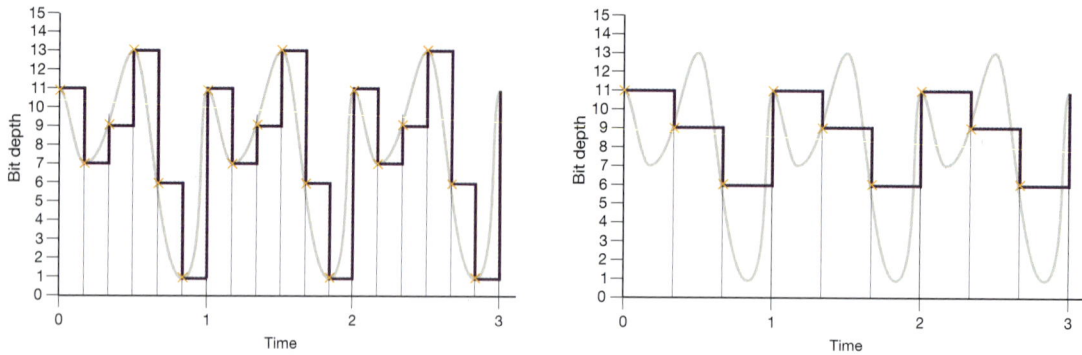

The **sample interval** is the amount of time between two samples. For example, if there are four samples a second, then the sample interval would be 0.25 seconds.

Factors affecting the size of a sound file and the quality of its playback

Sample rate: The number of samples taken in a second. This is measured in hertz (Hz), where

1 hertz = 1 sample per second

The more frequently the sound is sampled, the better the quality of playback. In the graph above, samples are taken every 1 unit of time – if we halved the sample interval, the wave would be more accurately represented.

Bit depth: The number of bits used to store each sample.

The more bits that are used, the better the accuracy of the recording. In the graph of a sound wave on the previous page, the bit depth on the Y axis has 16 different amplitudes that a sample can be recorded at. It could be more accurately represented with 32 or more points, but this would increase the number of bits that must be stored for each sample.

Sample size: The number of seconds over which the sample was taken.

Example 2: Calculating the size of a sound file

The file size of a sound file = sample rate × bit depth × seconds

A sample rate of 44.1kHz is typically used for CD audio, with a bit depth of 16 bits per sample.

So the file size of a sample lasting 5 seconds would be

$(44.1 \times 1000 \times 16 \times 5) / 8$ bytes

$= 44\,100 \times 16 \times 5 / 8$ bytes

$= 441\,000$ bytes

$= 441\,000 / 1024$

$= 430.7$ kiB

Q22 Calculate the file size in bytes of a 10 second radio jingle, using a sample rate of 8,000Hz and a bit depth of 16 bits

2.7 – Compression

When data is transmitted across the internet it will go through many different physical links between routers. The connection from a computer or a LAN into the internet is likely to be the slowest part of this route, as you probably know from experience. At home you may have quite a slow network connection and it may take a while for images, audio or video to load.

One way of speeding up the rate at which files can be transmitted across the internet is to compress them to make them smaller. Smaller files take less time to transmit over a network.

Understanding how compression affects files is important as the type of compression selected will affect how the image looks or the audio track sounds. The final use of the file will dictate how much you can compress it and still have a file that is useable.

To summarise, compression is used in order to:

- reduce the amount of storage needed on a computer to save files
- allow large files to be transmitted as an email attachment; many email servers limit the size of a file that can be sent, and compression can reduce the file size allow to allow users to send the file
- allow a file to be transmitted in less time, owing to the smaller file size

Lossy compression

Lossy compression is a data encoding method where files are compressed by removing some of the detail. For example, photographs can be stored using fewer colours so fewer bits are needed per pixel. This type of compression is used to compress images, audio files and video files, where it is easy to recognise an image or sound clip even if some data is missing.

A bitmap image (.bmp) is an uncompressed version of an image. If you save the same photograph as a JPEG file then it is still a high quality image with a colour depth of 24 bits but some of the data is lost where it is unlikely to be noticed.

Reduction of file size can also be achieved by reducing the colour depth from 24-bit colour, to 8-bit colour, for example. The human eye can tell the difference at this stage. You will see solid blocks of colour instead of gradual transitions in the photograph.

Here is a section of a photograph which has been altered to show the difference:

24-bit colour

8-bit colour

Lossy compression formats are show below:

Type	File suffix	Compression Type	Explanation
JPEG	.jpg	Lossy	Good for photographs. Colour depth = 24 bits, RGB, 16.7 million different colours
Windows Media Player	.wmv	Lossy	Uses Windows Media compression
MP3	.mp3	Lossy	Audio files: Designed for downloading music from the internet. In MP3 format you could fit 120 songs on a CD.
MPEG-1	.mpg	Lossy	Video files: Suitable for small low-resolution sequences on CD
MPEG-2	.mp2	Lossy	Video files: Suitable for full-screen, high resolution video on DVD

Lossless compression

This is a data encoding method where files are compressed but no data is lost – an essential factor for text and data files. For example, bank records must keep all of the data; you cannot transmit a bank statement and miss out a few zeros because they don't matter too much!

Lossless compression could be used to compress data files, for example by 'zipping' them using a utility program such as WinZip, before attaching them to an email.

The following table shows different file types and file extensions used for lossless compression formats:

Type	File suffix	Compression Type	Explanation
Graphic Interchange Format	.gif	Lossless	Colour depth = 8 bits (only 256 colours) Transparency for each pixel only has one option, on or off
Portable Network Graphic	.png	Lossless	Colour depth = 24 bits, RGB, 16.7 million different colours Degree of transparency for each pixel can have multiple levels
FLAC	.flac	Lossless	Lossless music. When compressed it still contains all the original audio information.
ZIP	.zip	Lossless	Used to compress files and folders for archiving or sharing.

Exercises

1. (a) Add the following two 8-bit binary numbers.   [2]

    0 0 1 1 0 1 0 1
    1 0 0 1 1 1 0 1

    (b) Explain what is meant by an overflow error when adding two 8-bit binary numbers. [2]

2. The number 73 could be a denary number or a hex number.

    (a) If 73 is a hex number, calculate its value as a denary number.

    You **must** show your working.   [2]

    (b) If 73 is a denary number, calculate its value as a hex number.

    You **must** show your working.   [2]

3. (a) Convert the binary number 10110110 to denary, showing your working.   [2]
    (b) Convert the denary number 175 to binary, showing your working.   [2]

4. (a) Convert the denary number -32 to two's complement.   [3]

    (b) Convert the two's complement binary number 11011011 to denary.   [3]

5. An arithmetic right shift of one place is applied to the number 10110100.
    (a) State the result after the arithmetic right shift has been applied.   [1]
    (b) State the result which would have occurred if a logical right shift had been used. [1]

6. (a) Explain why data is stored in computers in a binary format.   [2]

    (b) In the ASCII character set, the character codes for three capital letters are given below.

Letter	ASCII character code
A	65
N	78
R	82

    (i) Explain how the ASCII character set is used to represent text in a computer.   [2]
    (ii) Convert the word RAN into binary using the ASCII character set.   [4]

7. A digital camera stores image files that require 3 mebibytes each.

    Calculate the amount of storage space that would be required to store 1024 images. Give your answer in gibibytes.

    You must show your working.   [2]

8. Files are often compressed before they are sent over the internet.

   (a) State what is meant by compression. [1]

   (b) State **two** advantages of compressing files before sending them over the internet. [2]

9. (a) The colour depth of an image is defined as the number of bits used to store each pixel.

      How many bits per pixel are required to store a greyscale image with 256 shades of grey? [1]

   (b) The resolution of an image is the number of pixels that make up an image.

      Explain the effect of increasing the resolution of an image. [3]

   (c) A camera takes images using a colour depth of 16 bits. It is set to a resolution of 10 megapixels.

      Calculate the file size in mebibytes of a image taken using this resolution. [2]

10. When recording sound digitally, two factors influence the quality of the recording: **sample rate** and **bit depth**.

    (a) (i) Sample rate is measured in hertz, where 1 hertz = 1 sample per second.

           Explain what is meant by a sample rate of 30kHz. [2]

        (ii) Explain what is meant by a resolution of 16 bits per sample. [2]

    (b) A 30-second advertising jingle is created using a sample rate of 40kHz and a bit depth of 16 bits.

        Calculate the size of the sound file. [4]

2

Section 3

Computers

Objectives

3

- Understand the von Neumann stored program concept
- Understand the role of main memory (RAM), CPU (control unit, arithmetic logic unit, registers), clock, address bus, data bus, control bus in the fetch-decode execute cycle
- Understand the role of secondary storage and the ways in which data is stored on devices, including magnetic, optical and solid state
- Understand the concept of an embedded system and what embedded systems are used for
- Understand the purpose and functionality of an operating system including file management, process management, peripheral management and user management
- Understand the purpose and functionality of utility software (file repair, backup, data compression, disk defragmentation and anti-malware)
- Understand the importance of developing robust software and methods of identifying vulnerabilities including audit trails and code reviews
- Understand the characteristics and purposes of low-level and high-level programming languages
- Understand how an interpreter differs from a compiler in the way it translates high-level code into machine code

3.1 – Computer architecture

Basic computer system model

A computer system is made up of hardware and software. Hardware is any physical component that makes up a computer. Software is any program that runs on a computer.

Computer systems are all around us. They are not just the PCs on a desk but include mobile phones, cash machines, supermarket tills and the engine management systems in a modern-day car.

The diagram below shows the basic model of a computer system.

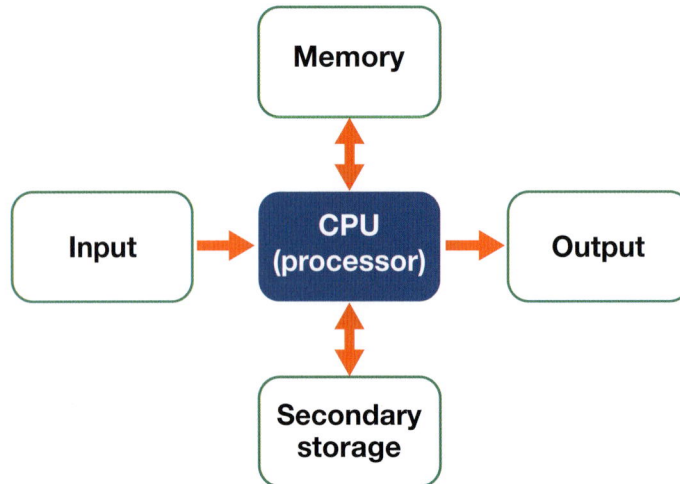

All computer systems must have a **central processing unit** (**CPU**), also called simply the processor, and at least one **input device** that gets data from the real world. This could be a mouse and keyboard on a conventional PC, a magnetic door sensor in a burglar alarm or the microphone on a mobile phone.

Input devices take real world data and convert it into a form that can be stored on a computer. The input from these devices is processed and the computer system will generate outputs. The **output device** could be, for example, a conventional computer screen, an actuator that opens or closes a greenhouse window, or the speaker that produces sound on a phone.

The computer must have **main memory** (primary storage), used for holding instructions currently being executed and data that is being used.

Any computer system will have these four basic components.

The fifth component is **secondary storage**. The computer system may need to use stored data to perform the processing and, as a result of processing input, may generate data that is then stored. Storage devices such as hard drives can hold large amounts of data including databases, text documents, programs, music files and photographs.

> **Q1** Name **three** input, output and storage devices.

Von Neumann architecture

With the very first computers, it was not possible to store programs, and programs were generally input by setting switches. John Von Neumann developed the concept of the **stored program computer** in the 1940s. The **Von Neumann** architecture used the idea of holding both programs and data in memory. Data would then move between the memory unit and the processor.

Common components and their function

The Central Processing Unit (CPU) of a computer is the hardware that executes programs and manages the rest of the hardware. Think of the CPU as the brain of the computer. Just as your brain contains parts that remember things, parts that think and parts that make the rest of your body operate, the CPU does the same for the computer. The computer also contains main memory. Main memory is either **Random Access Memory** (**RAM**) or **Read Only Memory** (**ROM**).

RAM is **volatile** memory. This means it will lose any data or programs that it stores when the power is turned off. ROM is **non-volatile** memory. This means that the instructions are written to it by the manufacturer. After this, no more instructions or data can be added, making it read only.

The CPU is able to read instructions and data from RAM and ROM in the same way.

Components of the CPU

The processor responds to and processes the instructions that run the computer. It contains the **Arithmetic Logic Unit** (**ALU**), **Control Unit** (**CU**) and **registers**.

The CPU sits on a motherboard which also contains a **clock** and the main memory.

Arithmetic and Logic Unit (ALU)

The ALU carries out the following functions:

- **Logical operations**: These include AND, OR and NOT
- **Shift operations**: The bits in a computer word can be shifted left or right by a certain number of places
- **Arithmetic operations**: These include addition, subtraction, multiplication and division.

Control unit

The Control Unit coordinates all the activities taking place inside the CPU. Its functions may be summarised as follows:

- It controls the execution of instructions in the correct sequence
- It decodes instructions
- It regulates and controls processor timing using regular pulses from the system **clock**
- It sends and receives control signals to and from other devices within the computer.

Registers

The CPU contains very fast memory locations known as **registers**. Some of these are specialist registers, such as the program counter (PC) which stores the location of the next instruction to be executed. Other registers are general purpose registers. These are used by the programmer to store results from calculations.

3

Clock

The system clock controls processor timing, switching between zero and one at rates exceeding several million times per second. It synchronises all CPU operations. See clock speed on page 55.

The system bus

The program instructions and data move between the main memory and the processor using internal connections called buses. There are three buses used, the address bus, control bus and data bus.

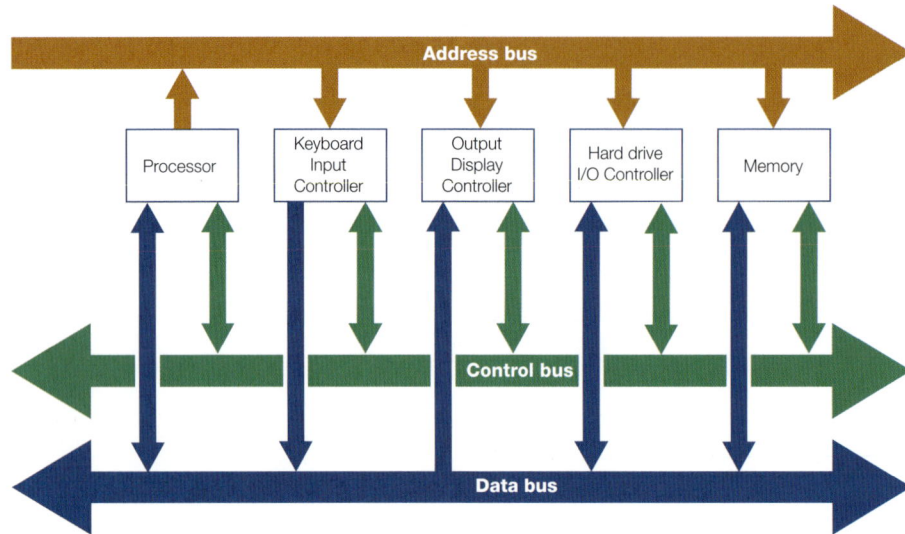

The following occurs if the CPU wants to request data from RAM.

- The CPU first copies the memory address it is requesting onto the address bus.
- The CPU then sets the control bus to show that it is waiting for data.
- The data is then copied from RAM onto the data bus.
- The control bus is set to ready.
- The CPU is then able to read the data from the data bus.

> **Q2** Explain how clock speed affects the performance of a computer.

> **Q3** Describe how buses are used when the CPU needs to read data from RAM.

3.2 – Fetch-Decode-Execute cycle

When a program is to be run (executed) on a computer it first has to be loaded into main memory. From here it can be accessed by the processor, which runs each instruction in turn. When the program is loaded, the processor is given the start address of where it is held in main memory.

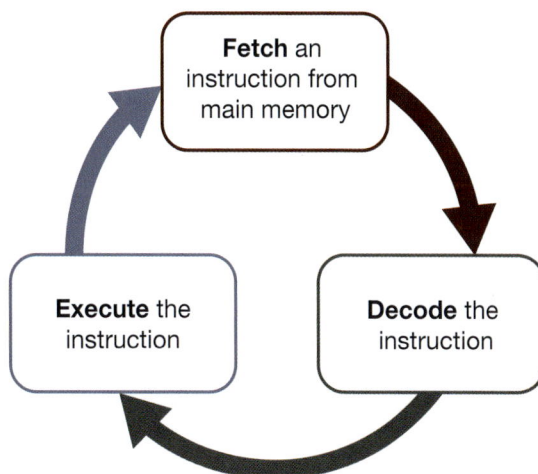

To run the program, the processor fetches an instruction, decodes it and then executes it. The processor executes one instruction at a time. This is called the **Fetch-Decode-Execute cycle**, or simply the **Fetch-Execute cycle**.

In the **fetch** part of the cycle:

- The address of the next instruction to be executed is fetched from a register (a special, super-fast memory location in the processor) where it is held
- The instruction at the address is fetched from memory and copied into a register ready to be decoded
- This register is incremented so it points to the next instruction to be fetched

In the **decode** part of the cycle:

- The Control Unit decodes the instruction

In the **execute** part of the cycle:

- The instruction is executed. Depending on what the instruction is, this could, for example, involve fetching data from memory and loading or adding it into a register, or jumping to another instruction in the program.

Clock speed

All processor activities begin on a clock pulse, although some activities may take more than one clock cycle to complete. One clock cycle per second = 1 hertz (Hz), and clock speed is measured in gigahertz (GHz), one billion cycles per second. Typical speeds for a PC are between 2 and 4 GHz. The greater the clock speed, the faster instructions will be executed.

Embedded systems

An embedded system is a small computer built into a piece of equipment designed to perform a specific function. Examples of items that use this technology include: vehicles, cameras, medical equipment, aircraft, vending machines, ovens, fridges, mobile phones, satellite navigation devices, televisions, digital clocks and lifts.

Characteristics of an embedded system

The main characteristics of an embedded system are reliability and minimal resources such as ROM, timers, sensors and actuators.

The program which controls the equipment is held in ROM and cannot be changed. It is typically written in a machine-efficient language so that it uses the minimum amount of memory and executes as fast as possible. Assembly language may be used for some critical parts of the program.

Embedded systems often don't use an operating system, or use a very limited one. Unlike a desktop computer, the embedded operating system and programs don't have to be loaded when the machine is switched on, as they are held in ROM. Embedded systems have very simple user interfaces, such as the buttons on a microwave oven or washing machine. Some embedded systems have no user interface. Other embedded systems have sensors designed to measure external stimuli and react accordingly. For example, a central heating system may use buttons and sliders to make the heating switch on at certain times of day, on different days, and maintain a chosen temperature.

3.3 – Secondary storage

We all want to store files for a long period of time. We keep photographs, projects, music, films, letters and spreadsheets on our computers. We also expect our programs to be there when we switch the computer on. This long term storage is usually called secondary storage (primary storage is the main memory). **Secondary storage** refers to hard disk drives (HDDs), optical disks and more recently, Solid State Drives (SSDs).

Secondary storage devices

Secondary storage is non-volatile, generally holds much more data than main memory and is relatively inexpensive per unit of storage. However, secondary storage technologies tend to have slower access speeds than main memory.

There are three different technologies that are usually used to make secondary storage. These are **magnetic disks**, **solid state** devices, and **optical** devices.

Each of these different technologies differ in terms of cost, capacity, access speed, portability, durability and reliability.

Magnetic disks

Magnetic disks are read with a moving head inside the disk drive. Moving parts make these media quite slow to read from or write to and also make the disk more susceptible to damage. This is in contrast to solid state media (SSD) which have no moving parts. Magnetic media are also vulnerable to magnetic fields.

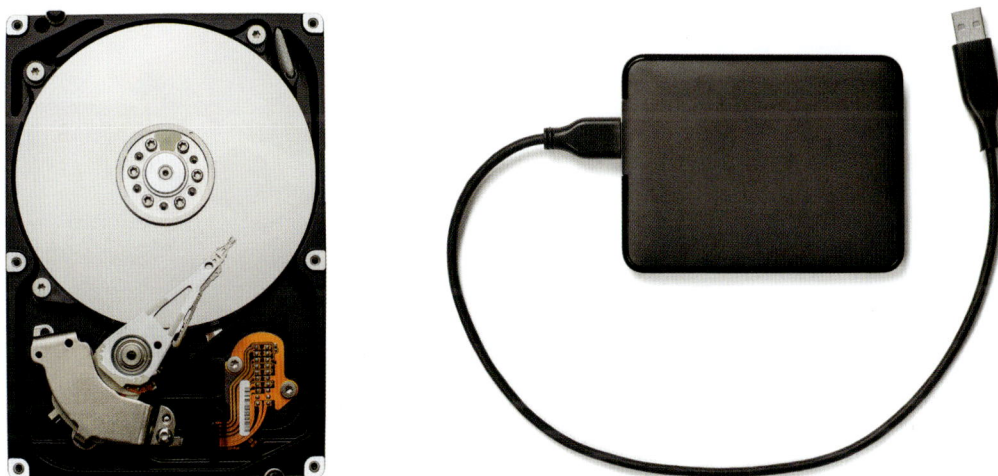

A hard disk uses rigid rotating platters coated with magnetic material. Ferrous (iron) particles on the disk are polarised to become either a north or south state. This represents 0 and 1. The disk is divided into tracks in concentric circles, and each track is subdivided into sectors. The disk spins very quickly at speeds of up to 10,000 RPM. Like a record player, a drive head (similar to the needle on a record player arm) moves across the disk to access different tracks and sectors. Data is read or written to the disk as it passes under the drive head. When the drive head is not in use, it is parked to one side of the disk in order to prevent damage from movement. A hard disk may consist of several platters, each with its own drive head.

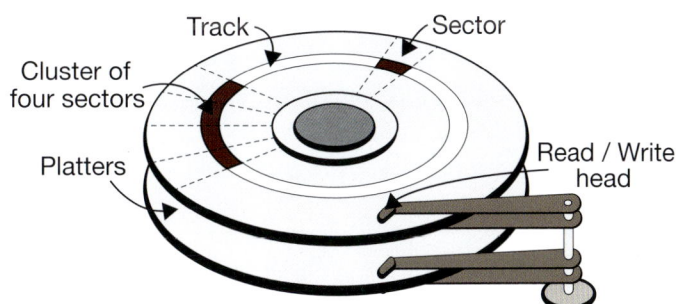

Magnetic disk drives can be either internal or portable (connected to the computer using a USB port).

Although hard disks are less portable than optical or solid state media, their huge capacity makes them very suitable for desktop purposes. Smaller, denser surface areas spinning under the read/write heads mean that newer disks have capacities of several tebibytes.

Solid state devices

Solid State Drives (**SSD**) have no moving parts and don't rely on magnetic properties, so are unaffected by magnetic fields. They are often referred to as **flash memory**/**storage**. They are typically very fast to access, but not as fast as RAM.

Solid state technology is also used in flash drives (memory sticks) and memory cards (e.g. SD and micro SD as used in cameras). Solid state technology is now also employed in many laptops and tablets as well as in mobile phones and other portable devices. The small size and reliability are key features in such devices which need to be portable and also have minimum drain on their internal batteries.

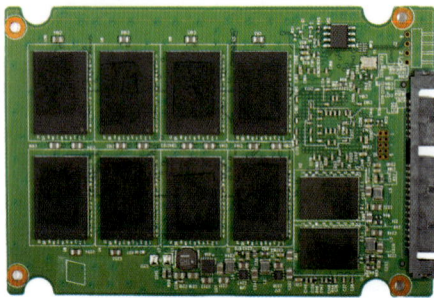

Hard drive

USB stick

Micro SD card

SD card

Solid state devices such as SSDs, memory sticks and memory cards all use flash memory. They are built from special types of transistors that do not lose their state when the power is switched off. There are two types of flash memory, NOR and NAND, which are wired in parallel and series respectively.

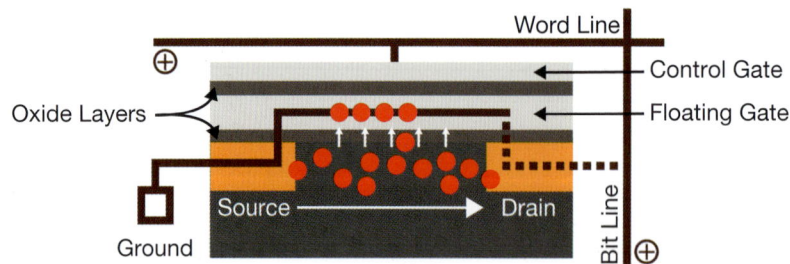

Flash memory storing one bit of information

Both types of SSD use electrical circuits to persistently store data. When a charge is applied to the bit line, electrons are pushed into the floating gate. This prevents the current from flowing through the transistor, causing the bit to store a 0. When the electrons are removed from the floating gate, the current flows through the transistor making the bit read a 1.

> **Q4** Which are cheaper, HDDs or SSDs? Is there a big difference in price?
> Research differences using an online electronics shop.

Optical devices

Optical devices make use of optical media including CDs (compact discs), DVDs (digital versatile discs) and Blu-ray discs.

Optical discs come in three different formats: read-only, recordable (once) or rewriteable (many times). Films and music are distributed via read only discs which are 'pressed' with the pits and lands that encode the data when they are manufactured.

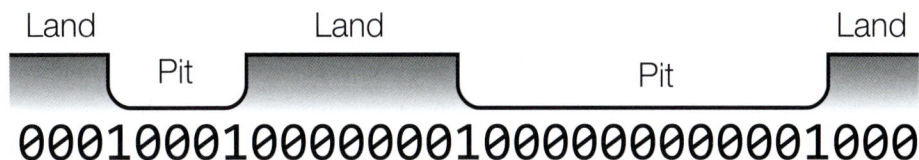

```
00010001000000001000000000001000
```

Bits stored on the surface of an optical disc

An optical disc works by using a low-powered laser to read the disc by bouncing light onto its surface, which is covered in pits and lands. At the point where a pit starts or ends, light is scattered and therefore not reflected so well. A land, and the bottom of a pit reflects the light well. Non-reflective and reflective areas are read as 1s and 0s. There is only one single track on an optical disk, arranged as a tight spiral. A recordable disc uses a higher powered laser to change the reflective properties of a disc and thus make lands and pits.

A CD holds about 650MB of data, a DVD holds around 9GB of data, whereas a Blu-ray disc holds around 50GB. Although these discs do not vary in physical size, their added capacity is owing to the shorter wavelength in the laser they use. This creates much smaller pits, enabling a greater number to fit in the same space along the track and also means that the track can be more tightly wound, and therefore much longer.

3

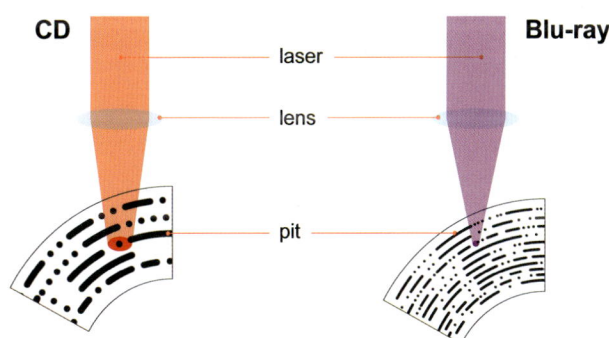

Optical discs are easily portable and carried in cases. However, if they get scratched the data cannot be read. This makes them typically less reliable than hard drives and solid state devices. By contrast, they are very cheap. For instance, a 50GB Blu-ray disc storing a film will cost under £1 to produce. A similar capacity flash drive might cost more than £5.

Q5 Describe the way in which data is stored on devices using each of the following methods:

- Magnetic
- Optical
- Solid state

3.4 – Operating systems

The operating system is a group of programs that manages the computer's resources. One feature of most operating systems that you will already be familiar with is the graphical user interface (GUI). This is the part of the operating system that allows the user to interact with it through the use of icons, windows, menus and pointers.

Operating systems are also responsible for other functions including:

- File management
- User management
- Process management
- Peripheral management

File management

A file system is normally organised into folders and subfolders for easy user navigation and usage. These folders contain files which could be software programs, databases, documents and many other types of file.

Name ^	Type	Size
Computer Science	File folder	
English	File folder	
Geography	File folder	
History	File folder	
Maths	File folder	
Science	File folder	
School Year	Text Document	183 KB
Timetable	Microsoft Word Document	91 KB

File management systems:

- enable a user to create, name, save, modify, copy, delete and move files and folders
- enable a user to search for a particular file
- keep track of location of files on the storage device so that they can be retrieved when needed
- keep track of the free space available where files can be stored
- enable users to restore deleted files
- prevent conflicts when two users on a network attempt to modify the same file
- maintain access rights to files

User management

User management enables a network administrator to allocate accounts and set different access rights for different users. Administration software can also identify all the users currently on the network, manually log out users and monitor when and for how long each user is logged in over a period of time.

The user management system allows the administrator to set default logout times based on inactivity.

Process management

A computer processor is able to run one **process** at a time. However, most users want to run multiple processes at the same time, such as a word-processor, web browser, calculator or game. To do this, a **multi-tasking** operating system is used. This manages each process so that it has a small amount of time running on the CPU before the next process gets a chance to run. By rapidly switching between the processes that are running on the CPU, the user perceives all the processes to be running at the same time. If the processor isn't capable of processing all the instructions fast enough, then one or more programs may appear to temporarily freeze.

Processes are in a number of states when they are run.

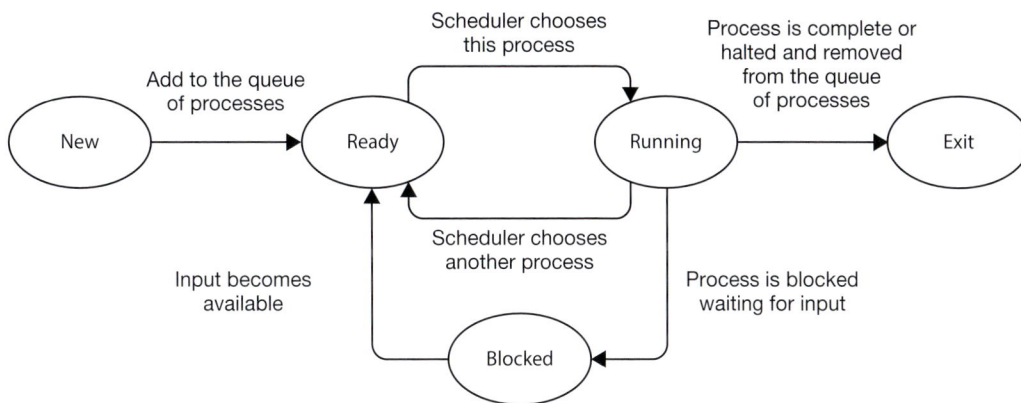

When you open a program the following happens:

1. A **new** process is added to the queue of processes. The program instructions and data are loaded into RAM.
2. The program is now **ready** to be run. However, there will currently be another process running and other processes that are currently ready.
3. After a short period of time, the scheduler chooses this process to run. It is now in the **running** state.
4. Once the process has been running for a short interval, the scheduler may choose to run a different process. In this case, it will put the process back to the **ready** state. Alternatively, whilst running the process may be waiting for an input. For example, when a word processor is running, it may be waiting for the user to type a letter on the keyboard. The process is **blocked** whilst it is waiting for input. Once the input arrives, the process then becomes **ready** again.
5. Finally, when the program has finished processing everything, or the user aborts or quits the program, it is removed from the queue of processes and has **exited**.

Peripheral management

Peripherals are any computer hardware components that are not part of the main computer unit (CPU and RAM). This includes input, output and storage devices. For some of these, the term peripheral makes sense; the keyboard and monitor, for example, are outside the main computer casing, but storage is not so obvious. Although a hard drive is usually inside the computer casing, it is still considered a peripheral as it is outside the processor and main memory combination. Storage devices such as portable hard drives, memory cards and DVD drives are also peripherals.

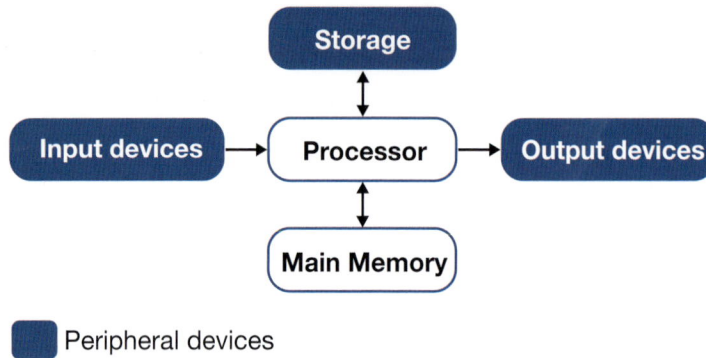

Peripheral devices

A function of the operating system is to manage these devices. When a user gives an instruction to print, the peripheral management function takes over and controls the sending of the data to be printed from memory to the device driver. Each input or output device has its own driver – a small program that acts as an interface between the computer and the device. A printer, for example, will have different device drivers for a PC and a Mac, and the correct driver has to be installed so that the computer can communicate with the printer.

Buffering is used to compensate for the difference in speeds between the rate that data is received for printing or streaming and the rate at which it can be printed or streamed. A data buffer is an area of RAM controlled by the operating system or peripheral management system. When you give a command to print a document, for example, all or part of the data to be printed is copied to the print buffer, and the print management system retrieves the data from the buffer and sends it to the printer. If the buffer is not big enough to hold all the data, the buffer will be refilled during printing as space becomes available.

> **Q7** Describe in detail four of the functions of a typical operating system. Explain why certain household devices may not need to have an operating system.

3.5 – Utility software

Strictly speaking, the operating system is the software that controls and manages the computer system but most operating systems also include programs called utilities. Utilities are not essential for the computer to work but either make it easier for the user to perform particular tasks, or provide housekeeping functionality. These utilities include:

- File repair
- Backup
- Data compression
- Disk defragmentation
- Anti-malware

File repair utilities

Sometimes files become **corrupted** which means they are damaged and cannot be opened. **File repair utilities** will recover as much useful data as possible from the file. They often are able to repair the files so they can be opened again. As file corruption is often specific to certain types of file, file repair utilities often focus on just certain types of file, for example, Microsoft Office documents or videos and photos.

Backup utilities

Backup software is designed to create a copy of files, folders or even an entire computer system.

Most computer systems have just one hard drive which stores all the user's files, software and operating system. If the drive breaks all the data could be lost. If a backup has been created, the computer and data can be **restored** to how it was when the backup was made.

A **full backup** will take an exact copy of all files on a computer. This takes a long time to complete as often many hundreds of gigabytes of files need to be backed up.

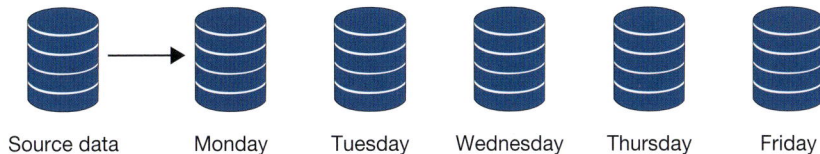

Source data	Monday	Tuesday	Wednesday	Thursday	Friday

Incremental backups first take a full backup. Then at regular time intervals an incremental backup is then made of just the files and folders that have changed since the previous backup. When restoring the files, the first full backup and all the increments are put together. Using incremental backups means that each individual backup is usually very fast. It also allows many snapshots of a drive to be taken without needing as much storage space as full backups.

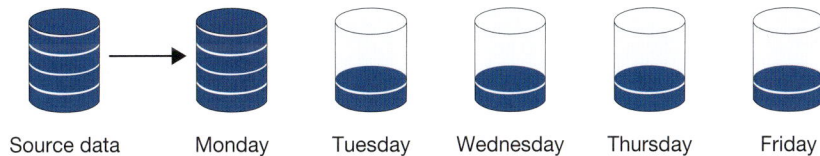

Source data	Monday	Tuesday	Wednesday	Thursday	Friday

Q8 Describe the backup schedule and method that is used within your school. You may need to ask your teacher or an IT technician for help.

3

Data compression software

Compression software such as WinZip will reduce the size of a file. There are two types of compression known as lossy and lossless; lossy compression can be used on photos where some detail is lost but this will be undetectable when viewed on screen. Lossless compression is used on text files, where it has to be possible to restore the file exactly.

Zipped or compressed files can be transmitted much more quickly over the internet. Sometimes there is a limit to the size of a file which can be transmitted – if you have a 15 MiB document, you will not be able to email it to a friend if there is a 10 MiB limit on the attachments they can receive. Even if they can receive the file, it may take several minutes to download if they do not have a broadband connection.

A further advantage of compressing files using a data compression utility such as WinZip is that several files can be compressed into a single zip file. They can then be transmitted, moved or stored as a single compressed file rather than as several separate files.

Defragmentation software

The file management utility in Windows makes the secondary storage area look like a nicely organised filing cabinet but it doesn't really look like this. Files are stored on the hard disk in blocks wherever there is space. If you have a big file it might get split up into segments so it can be stored in the available gaps. After a while, thousands of files are stored in segments all over the disk. Files have become 'fragmented'. This makes file access inefficient as, to access one file, the drive head may have to move to many locations to read it.

The **disk defragmenter** moves the separate parts of the files around so that they can be stored together, which makes them quicker to access. The defragmenter also groups all the free disk space together so that new files can be stored in one place. This optimises disk performance.

Before disk is defragmented, the disk contains lots of files, stored all over the disk.

A new file has to be saved in three different parts of the disk. Makes reading the file slower.

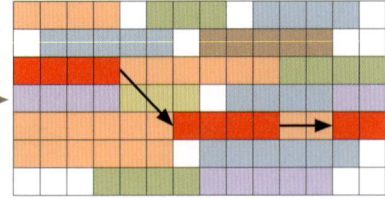

After defragmenting, the disk looks like this:

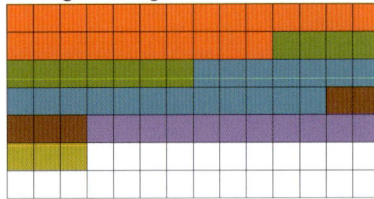

A new file can be saved in one place so it speeds up read access

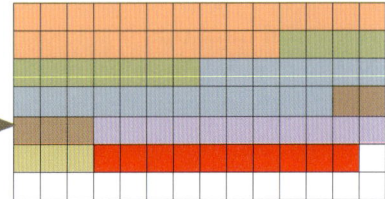

Note that a solid state drive or solid state media does not need to be defragmented. Defragging has no benefit as on a solid state drive as the access time of each block is the same no matter where it is placed. This is because there are no moving parts. Running defragmentation software on solid state drives may shorten their life.

Anti-malware software

Malware is malicious software which causes deliberate harm to a computer. Common types of malware include viruses, Trojan horses, spyware and ransomware.

Anti-malware software detects malware and then removes it from a computer system. Malware will have common patterns in the code that runs or the type of activities it carries out. These signatures are detected by the anti-malware software. Once detected, the files are placed in quarantine where they cannot be run. The user can then delete the files.

Anti-malware software includes antivirus software (which detects viruses) and spyware detection software which find spyware.

The anti-malware software may be able to remove any issues that the malware created. In some cases, such as ransomware, the malware has encrypted the storage device. It is usually impossible for any software to undo the encryption. Only the password (decryption key) will be able to do this. For these situations the computer system will need to be recovered from the latest backup made.

3.6 – Robust software

Developing robust software

When software is developed, it should be robust. This means that it is able to withstand attacks and threats by hackers and malware. It must also be reliable for use by ordinary users and able to cope with accidental misuse.

When developing robust software, developers will use techniques such as:

- **Validation** – checking that input entered conforms to rules
- **Verification** – checking that data is correct, for example, by asking a user to enter it twice, or by verifying entered data with another source such as a database
- **Authentication** – using identification such as a swipe card, contactless ID or facial recognition.

Testing is a key part of the development of robust software. Consideration of all paths that can be taken in the software is important for making sure that every eventuality results in the correct processing output or error message.

Methods of identifying vulnerabilities

Two methods of identifying vulnerabilities are the use of code reviews and audit trails.

Code reviews

Code reviews allow for more robust programming code to be developed. One or more reviewers check the code once it has been completed. At least one of these reviewers should be someone who hasn't authored the code. The use of reviewers has the following advantages:

- Defects are more likely to be found
- Better quality code should result
- Better solutions and algorithms can be found
- More than one person becomes responsible for the code
- There is a transfer of knowledge to the other reviewers, so more people fully understand how the code works

Audit trails

System logs keep key information about the state of a computer before a software issue occurs. They are helpful in troubleshooting errors.

Audit logs help to give a fuller record of the activity that occurred when using a computer or software. This is used when making sure that company policies and laws have been followed, this is known as **compliance**. The use of audit logs also helps to reduce misuse. After all, if users know that all their activity will be logged, they are less likely to misuse software or a computer system. Audit logs are helpful in detecting misuse. They are likely to record:

- Who was using the computer (username or ID)
- The event that occurred and the events leading up to it
- Device details (Operating system and system configuration)
- The IP address

> **Q9** Describe the information that a school's Information Management System (IMS) should record in an audit log.

3.7 – Programming languages

Programming languages can be broadly divided into two categories:

- low-level languages (processor-specific assembly languages and machine code)
- high-level languages such as Python, Visual Basic, C# and many others

The binary instructions that run on a computer are known as machine code. This code is specific to the processor that it is being written for. To write code at the processor level we use assembly language. There are lots of different assembly languages; one for each different processor architecture. The code is written using mnemonics, abbreviated text commands such as LDA (LOAD), STO (STORE), and ADD.

Human beings find it easier to write programs in languages that are suited to the type of problem they are trying to solve and that look more like normal languages, and high-level languages were created for this. There are many different programming languages to suit different types of problem. For example, you might use Visual Basic to write a forms-based data processing application or you might use Python for data analysis.

Differences between high-level and low-level languages

Type of language	Example	Characteristics	Sample instructions

High-level language	Python, Visual Basic, C#	Independent of hardware (portable)
		Translated using a compiler or interpreter
		One statement translates into many
			`rate = 3.02`
			`used = 5672`
			`billAmount = rate * used`

Low-level language	Assembly language	Translated using an assembler One statement translates into one machine code instruction	`LDA #34` `STO &39FC`
	Machine code	Executable binary code produced by a compiler, interpreter or assembler	`1010100011010101` `0100100101010101`

High-level languages such as Python and Visual Basic have the following features, which are not available in low-level languages:

- Selection and iteration constructs such as IF… ELIF… ELSE, FOR loops and WHILE loops
- Identifiers using an unlimited number of alphabetic and numeric characters and some special characters means that variable names can be made meaningful, for example `averageTemperature`, `eveningRate`
- Data structures such as arrays, lists and records
- Subprograms such as functions and procedures allow code to easily be reused

Low-level languages have a much more limited number of programming constructs, with selection and iteration being performed using 'compare and branch' instructions. These languages are harder to learn, more time-consuming to code and more difficult to debug.

Advantages and use of high-level languages

Most software is developed using a high-level language for the following reasons:

- High-level languages are relatively easy to learn and much faster to program in.
- The program code can be compiled or interpreted for use on different processors. This means that the code only needs to be written once to work on many different types of computer
- Since statements written in these languages look a bit like English or maths, they are easier to read and understand, debug and maintain.
- Complex assignment statements such as:
  ```
  x = (math.sqrt(b**2 - 4 * a * c)) / (2 * a)
  ```
  mean that a program in a high-level language is generally much closer to the algorithm for solving the problem, and therefore much more straightforward to code

Advantages and use of low-level languages

Assembly language is often used in embedded systems such as the computer systems that control a washing machine, vehicle, set of traffic lights or a robot. It has the following features which make it suitable for this type of application:

- It gives the programmer complete control over the system components so it can be used to **control and manipulate specific hardware components**
- Very efficient code can be written for a particular type of processor, so it will occupy **less memory** and **execute faster** than a compiled high-level language

Differences between assembly code and machine code language

Machine code is the code executed by the processor, and consists only of 0s and 1s. Each type of processor has its own machine code instruction set. An assembly program needs to be translated to machine code using an **assembler** before it can be executed.

Translating high-level languages

Compiler

A **compiler** translates a program written in a high-level programming language into machine code. This is a more complex process than translating assembly code as a single instruction can result in many machine code instructions. Different compilers for a particular language are needed for different types of processor.

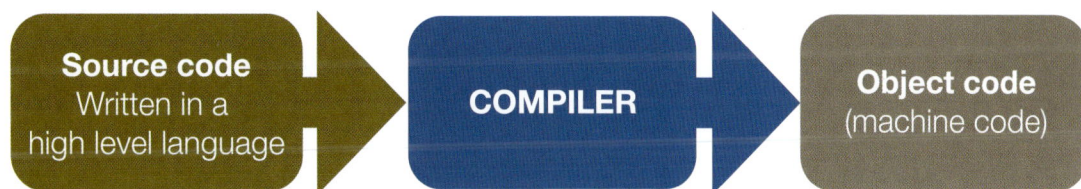

The code written by the programmer is known as **source code**, and the machine code produced by the compiler is called **object code**. When you buy commercial software you are buying the object code, and you do not need the compiler in order to run the software.

For the developer, this has the advantage that someone buying the software cannot see the source code or copy it.

Interpreter

An interpreter is also used to translate high-level language code into machine code. Unlike a compiler, it translates each line of source code and then executes it, and no object code is produced. You must have the interpreter installed on your computer in order to run the software.

A long, complex program will take considerably more time to execute if it is being interpreted. For example, if a loop is performed 10,000 times, the lines within the loop are translated 10,000 times.

The distinction between a compiler and an interpreter is not completely clear-cut, however. Some languages such as Java, which is used in creating some smartphone apps, are compiled into an intermediate stage called bytecode. This can be interpreted and run on many different types of processor using an appropriate bytecode interpreter, so that the app can be viewed on any type of smartphone.

The table below compares compilers and interpreters:

Compiler	Interpreter
Translates the whole program to produce the executable object code	Translates and executes one line at a time
Compiled program executes faster as it is already in machine code	Interpreted programs take more time to execute because each instruction is translated before it is executed
Customers do not need to have the compiler installed on their computer to run the software	Customers must have the interpreter installed on their computer
Customers cannot see the actual source code when you distribute the program	Customers can see the source code and could copy it

Q10 Describe the benefits and drawbacks of using a low-level language compared to a high-level language.

Q11 Describe the benefits and drawbacks of using an interpreted language such as Python compared with a compiled language such as C#.

Exercises

1. Tick **one** box in each row to show whether each of the following statements is true or false. [5]

	True	False
The higher the clock speed, the faster a CPU is able to process each instruction		
The CPU fetches, decodes and executes instructions		
Registers on the CPU are slower to access than main memory such as RAM		
The CPU control unit is responsible for adding two numbers together		
The clock speed of a CPU is usually measured in gigahertz (GHz)		
In the von Neumann architecture, both program instructions and data are stored in RAM		

2. Give **two** examples where an embedded system is likely to be used. [2]

3. (a) Describe **three** advantages of solid state drives compared with hard disk drives. [3]

   (b) Give **one** reason why an organisation might choose a hard disk drive rather than a solid state drive for a file server. [1]

   (c) Describe briefly the operation of a solid state drive. [3]

   (d) Describe briefly the operation of a hard disk drive. [3]

   (e) Describe briefly the operation of an optical drive. [3]

3

4. State which **four** of the following tasks are carried out by the operating system. [4]

   - File management
   - Managing email
   - Process management
   - Web browsing
   - Sorting records in a database
   - Peripheral management
   - User management
   - Spellcheck processing

5. Describe how an operating system is able to manage multiple processes running at the same time if it only has one CPU. [4]

6. Harry complains that reading data from his hard disk has become very slow.

   (a) Explain **one** possible reason for this. [2]

   (b) Explain what action he should take to solve the reason you gave in part (a). [2]

7. Explain the purpose of each of the following utility programs.

   (a) File repair software. [2]

   (b) Backup software. [2]

   (c) Data compression software. [2]

   (d) Anti-malware. [2]

8. A games developer is creating a computer game for a games console.

   (a) Explain **one** advantage of using a high-level programming language when programming the game. [2]

   (b) Explain **one** situation where a low-level programming language may be used. [2]

   (c) Explain **one** advantage of using a compiled language for the game rather than an interpreted language. [2]

3

Section 4

Networks

Objectives

- Understand the reasons why computers are connected in a network
- Understand the different types of networks including LAN and WAN
- Be able to explain how the internet is structured including IP addressing and routers
- Know the characteristics of wired and wireless connectivity
- Understand how the characteristics of wired and wireless connectivity impact on performance (speed, range, latency and bandwidth).
- Know that network speeds are measured in bits per second such as kbps (kilobits per second), Mbps (megabits per second) and Gbps (gigabits per second).
- Be able to construct expressions involving file size, transmission rate and time
- Understand the role of and need for network protocols, including Ethernet, Wi-Fi, TCP/IP, HTTP, HTTPS, FTP, POP3, SMTP and IMAP
- Understand how the 4-layer TCP/IP model handles data transmission over a network including application, transport, internet and link layers
- Be able to describe different characteristics of network topologies including bus, star and mesh topologies
- Understand the importance of network security
- Know different ways of identifying network vulnerabilities, including penetration testing and ethical hacking
- Describe methods of protecting networks including access control, physical security and firewalls

4

4.1 – The Internet and networks

A computer network is a collection of computers linked together to facilitate communication and the sharing of resources. They may be connected either wired or wirelessly.

Local Area Networks (LANs)

A **Local Area Network** (**LAN**) usually covers a relatively small geographical area. It consists of a collection of computers and peripheral devices (such as printers) connected together, often on a single site. At school you probably have many different buildings inside the school site, with the school's LAN connecting the computers in all these buildings. A LAN is often owned and managed by a single person or organisation.

Wide Area Networks (WANs)

A **Wide Area Network** (**WAN**) is a collection of computers and networks connected together using resources supplied by a 'third party carrier' such as BT. It uses cables, telephone lines, satellites and radio waves to connect the components, which are usually spread over a wide geographical area.

WANs tend to be under collective or distributed ownership and are not necessarily owned by one organisation, owing to the extremely high cost of such a system. Some large and medium-sized organisations have their own private wide area networks or WANs. A group of government departments, NHS trusts or financial institutions might collectively own a wide area network.

A business with offices in London, Leeds, Bristol and York may lease WAN connections from a network service provider to connect the four office LANs together.

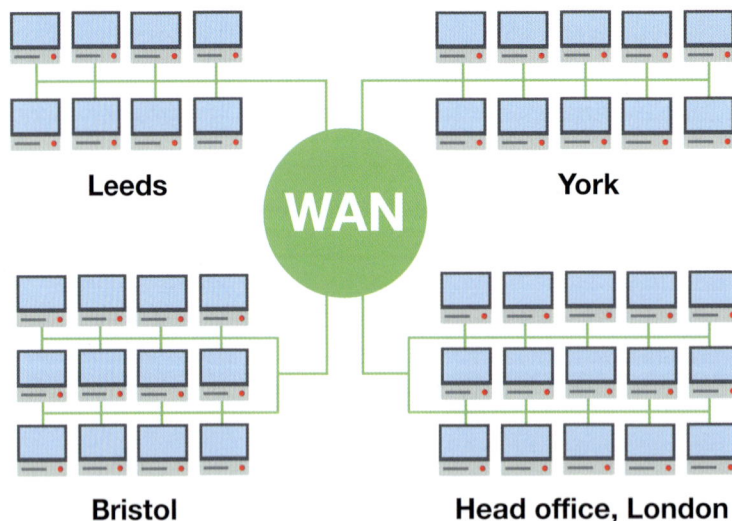

Benefits of networking computers

These are some of the benefits of networking computers belonging to a single organisation:

Sharing resources

- Folders and files can be stored on a file server so they can be accessed by authorised users from any computer on the network
- Peripheral devices such as printers and scanners can be shared
- Internet connection can be shared

Centralised management

- User profiles and security can all be managed centrally
- Software can be distributed across the network rather than having to install it on each individual computer
- All files can be backed up centrally

The disadvantages of networking computers include:

- If the file server goes down, no one can access their files or do any work
- Network faults could lead to loss of data
- As network traffic increases, performance degrades so accessing resources might be slow
- It is harder to make the system secure from hackers
- Viruses may be able to infiltrate the network and infect every computer
- The larger the network becomes, the more difficult it is to manage

The Internet

The largest and most famous wide area network in the world is the **internet**, a collection of inter-connected networks. It is a worldwide collection of computers and networks, not owned or managed by any one group of people. Anyone can access the internet.

The internet is not the same thing as the World Wide Web. Websites are stored on web servers connected to the internet, and each site has a unique web address so that it can be accessed. All information on the World Wide Web is stored in documents known as web pages. These pages are accessed using a program called a web browser such as Firefox, Edge or Google Chrome.

The Web is just one of the ways in which information is communicated over the internet. The internet, not the Web, is used for email and instant messaging.

IP addressing

Every networked computer or computing device in the world has a separate, unique IP address, although you will see later that a mobile device's IP address changes as it moves location. The current addressing system is called IPv4. An IPv4 address is typically written in dotted decimal digits, formatted as four 8-bit fields separated by full stops. Each 8-bit field represents a byte of the IPv4 address. IP stands for Internet Protocol and an IP version 4 address takes the form:

$$65.123.217.14$$

There are 4.3 billion IPv4 addresses and in 2020 there were over 30 billion connected devices. We have run out of IPv4 addresses so a new system, IPv6, is replacing it.

An IPv6 address is 128 bits long, (four times as long as an IPv4 address), arranged in eight groups of 16 bits each. Each group is four hexadecimal digits, separated by colons. The number of potential addresses that this allows is enough to address every atom on the surface of the planet. An example of an IPv6 address is:

BC43:71A6:0000:044C:3879:0000:55FD:286B

This may be shortened; for example groups of four zeros may be shortened to a single zero, so the above IP address could be written BC43:71A6:0:044C:3879:0:55FD:286B. All modern computers and mobile phones support both IPv4 and IPv6, and if you look at your device IP addresses you will probably see both.

Packet switching

Older analogue landlines work by making a dedicated connection between you and the person you are calling for the duration of the call. This is called **circuit switching**. This is fine for telephone calls, but there could never be enough lines for all the billions of people sending data across the internet.

This is where **packet switching** comes in.

Suppose you want to send a file of 3MB across the internet. The file is broken up into data 'packets' of around 512 bytes. Each packet is given a header containing:

- The IP (Internet Protocol) address it is going to
- The IP address it has come from
- The sequence number of the packet
- The number of packets in the whole communication
- Error checking data

Packets are then sent to their destination via the fastest route at the time, which may be different for each packet. They are reassembled in the right order when they arrive.

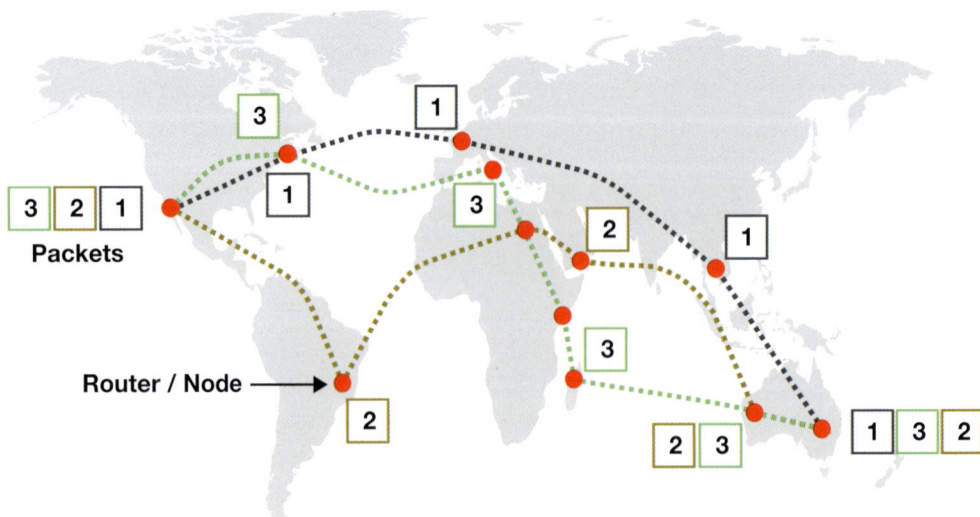

Routers

A router is designed to route data packets across a wide area network such as the internet. It is used for connecting networks. Each router in a network acts as a node and packets are passed from router to router to their destination somewhere on the internet. If a packet is destined for a computer in a LAN, it will typically be routed to a switch. Most home routers act as both a router and switch in one unit.

4.2 – Wired and wireless networks

Wired networks are connected using cables, whilst wireless networks are connected without.

Cabled networks tend to be more reliable and are capable of transferring data over a longer distance. They are more secure as a physical cable has to be connected to the network. Wireless connections, by contrast, are easier to connect devices to and more suited to portable devices such as smartphones and tablet computers.

The type of cable and particular standards used will have an impact on the performance of the connection. Performance is considered in terms of:

- **Range** – The distance between two points on the network
- **Latency** – The time taken for one packet of data to be transmitted between two points on the network
- **Bandwidth** – The amount of data that can be transmitted through the network. This is usually measured in **kilobits per second** (**kbps**), **megabits per second** (**Mbps**) or **gigabits per second** (**Gbps**)

The speed of a network connection can have multiple meanings. It could refer to the bandwidth, as a higher bandwidth means less time waiting to download a file. It also may refer to the latency, as a low latency will result in data taking less time to arrive at its destination. Finally, the speed of a network may refer to how much data is passing through it. For example, as more users use the school network the overall speed may slow down. However, each connection still has the same bandwidth and latency.

The following table shows how different characteristics are impacted by being wired or wireless.

	Cable type	Range	Latency	Bandwidth
Wireless	Wi-Fi 2.4 GHz	20 metres	Typically, higher latency	Up to 450 Mbps
	Wi-Fi 5 GHz	15 metres		Up to 1300 Mbps
Wired	Copper Ethernet cable	100 metres	Typically, lower latency	Typically, 100 Mbps
	Fibre optic cable	100 kilometres		Up to 10 Gbps

Notice how the newer Wi-Fi 5 GHz has less range and less ability to penetrate walls than Wi-Fi 2.4 GHz. However, it has a higher bandwidth. A modern router can use both frequencies.

Q1 A smart TV and smartphone need to connect to a home router. Explain which type of connection you would choose for each.

Network speed calculations

It is possible to work out how long a file will take to transmit based on the file size and transmission rate. When carrying out these calculations note that bandwidth and transmission rates are usually given in bits per second, whilst file sizes are usually in bytes. Therefore, any file size in bytes must first be converted to bits before using the formula.

$$\text{Transfer time (seconds)} = \frac{\text{file size (bits)}}{\text{transmission rate (bits per second)}}$$

Example

Chloe wants to download a 20 MiB file to her computer. Her connection is 10 Mbps. How long will the file take to download?

Convert the file size to bits: 20 MiB × 1024 × 1024 × 8 = 167 772 160 bits.

Convert the connection speed to bits: 10 Mbps = 10 × 1 000 000 = 10 000 000 bps.
(Note that connection speeds normally use kilo as 1000, mega as 1 000 000, giga as 1 000 000 000.)

Transfer time = 167 772 160 / 10 000 000 = 16.8 seconds.

Q2 Calculate how long it will take to transfer each of the following files.
(a) A 23 MiB file using a 50 Mbps connection.
(b) A 350 MiB audio file of a music album using a 1 Mbps connection.
(c) A 2 GiB video file using an 80 Mbps connection.

4.3 – Protocols and layers

If one computer transmits a stream of binary to another computer, the receiving end needs to know what protocol is being used. A protocol is the set of rules that define how devices communicate. A protocol will specify, for example:

- the format of data packets
- the addressing system
- the transmission speed
- error-checking procedures being used

Transmission Control Protocol / Internet Protocol (TCP/IP)

TCP/IP consists of two separate protocols. **TCP** is a standard that defines how messages are broken up into packets and reassembled at the destination. It also detects errors and resends lost packets. The **IP** protocol identifies the location of a device on the internet and routes the individual packets from source to destination via routers.

HyperText Transfer Protocol (HTTP) and HyperText Transfer Protocol Secure (HTTPS)

HTTP (HyperText Transfer Protocol) is used for accessing and receiving web pages in the form of HTML (Hypertext Markup Language) files on the internet. The protocol requests the web server to transmit the requested web page to the user's browser for viewing.

HTTPS (Hypertext Transfer Protocol Secure) encrypts the information so that it cannot be understood if it is hacked. Banks always use the HTTPS protocol.

Q3 What other websites might require the use of https ?

File Transfer Protocol (FTP)

FTP is a standard network protocol used when transferring computer files between a client and server on a computer network. FTP is faster than HTTP for transferring files. It requires users to log in with a username and password to transfer files.

Ethernet

Ethernet refers to a family of networking rules or protocols widely used in Local Area Networks.

It describes how devices should format data ready for transmission between computers on the same network.

- Similar to polite human conversation, nodes will wait until the connection is quiet before attempting to 'speak' or transmit
- Two nodes attempting to transmit simultaneously will stop and each wait a random period before reattempting

Ethernet systems divide data into frames, similar to internet packets. Each frame contains source and destination MAC addresses and error checking data. Faulty frames containing transmission errors are dropped or resent.

Wi-Fi

Wi-Fi (also known as Wireless LAN) is a set of wireless protocols which allow devices to be connected to a network wirelessly. The standard is also known as 802.11. The protocols set the different frequencies for transmission (typically 2.4GHz or 5GHz) along with how messages will be transmitted. Messages are split into frames that are very similar to Ethernet frames. Wi-Fi devices may be moved to somewhere with a poorer signal. This means that they are more likely to have errors in transmission. As a result, the Wi-Fi protocol is better at the way it deals with managing errors and resending the data frames.

4

Email protocols

Mail servers pass on or store emails until they are collected. You must log on to a mail server to collect mail.

Post Office Protocol (POP)

This is a widespread method of receiving email. Much like the physical version of a Post Office, **POP** receives and holds email for an individual until they pick it up. Periodically, you will check your mailbox on the server and download any mail, probably using POP. Since POP creates local copies of emails and deletes the originals from the server, the emails are tied to that specific device and can be viewed offline.

Internet Messaging Access Protocol (IMAP)

The Internet Message Access Protocol (**IMAP**) is an email protocol that stores email messages on a server but allows users to view and manipulate the messages as though they were stored locally on their own computers. Users can organise messages into folders, flag messages as urgent and save draft messages on the server. While the POP protocol assumes that your email is being accessed from only one application, IMAP allows simultaneous access by multiple clients. This is why IMAP is more suitable for you if you're going to access your email from different devices or if your messages are managed by multiple users.

POP	IMAP
Works best with only one computer to check your email.	You can use multiple computers and devices to check your email.
Your emails are downloaded and stored on the computer that you use.	Your emails are stored on the server and your devices synchronise with the server.
Sent email is stored locally on your computer and not on an email server.	Sent email stays on the server so you can access it from any device.

Simple Mail Transfer Protocol (SMTP)

SMTP is a protocol for sending e-mail messages between servers. Most e-mail systems that send mail over the internet use SMTP to send messages from one server to another; this is necessary if the sender and recipient have different email service providers. The messages can then be retrieved with an e-mail client using either POP or IMAP. Users typically use a program that uses SMTP for sending e-mail and either POP or IMAP for receiving e-mail.

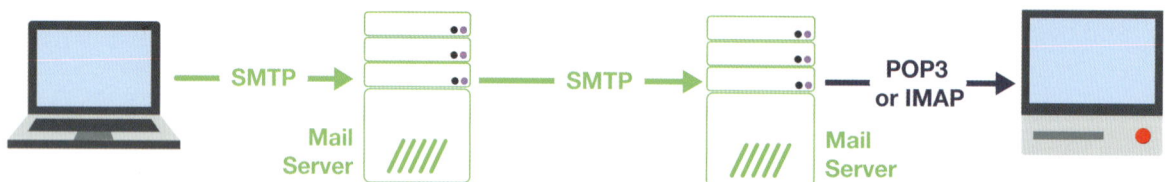

Network layers

The TCP/IP model consists of four layers, creating a modular design with each layer responsible for a small part of the communication process.

The advantage of this modular design is that it lets suppliers easily adapt the protocol software to different hardware and operating systems. For example, software for an Ethernet system can be adapted to an optical-fibre network by changing only the link layer – other layers are not affected.

Having different layers each performing a specified task means that products from different vendors can work together. A network software developer working on a new method of splitting the data into packets, for example, does not need to know how the tasks performed in other layers work.

The four layers of the TCP/IP stack are shown below.

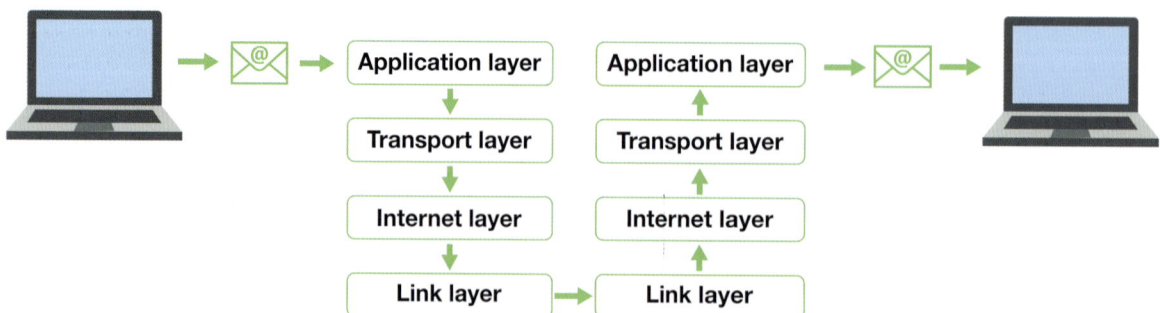

- At the top there is the **Application layer** which encodes the data being sent so that it will be understandable by the recipient. This means formatting data and adding an appropriate header according to a protocol being used, such as HTTP or FTP.

- Next there is the **Transport layer** which splits the data into packets and adds packet information such as packet number specifying that packet's order and the total number of packets so they can be reassembled correctly.

- The third layer is the **Internet layer** which attaches the IP address of the sender so the recipient will know who sent it. It also attaches the address of the host that is sending the data, and the destination IP address.
- The fourth layer is the **Link layer** which attaches the MAC addresses of the sender and the recipient, allowing the packet to be directed to a specific device on a local area network, for example.

At the receiving end, these data packets are passed back up the protocol stack.

4.4 – Network topologies

Computers can be connected together in different layouts, or topologies. The most commonly used topology in homes and schools is the star topology. You also need to be aware of the bus and mesh topologies.

Star topology

All of the computers have their own cable connecting them to a hub or switch, which routes messages to the correct computer. Hubs will send the message to all the connected computers, with each computer deciding if the message is for them. Switches will only send the message to the correct computer that the message was intended for.

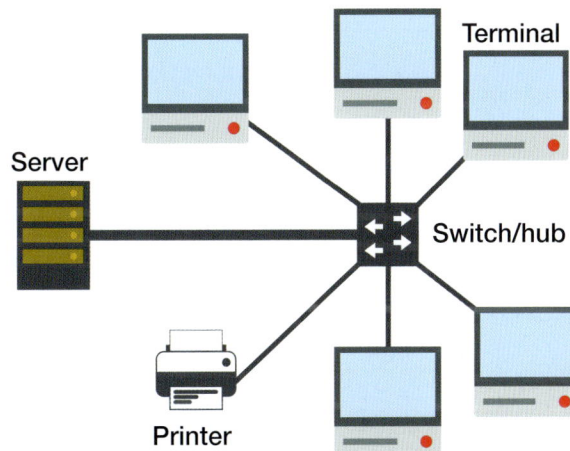

Advantages	Disadvantages
If one cable fails, the other workstations are not affected	Can be costly to install because there is a lot of cabling and extra hardware such as the switch
Consistent performance even when the network is heavily used	If the server or the central switch fails then the whole network goes down
Good security when a switch is used as data is received only by the node for which it is intended	

A star topology is often the layout of choice in a school or office because it is the most reliable of the topologies.

Bus topology

Historically, computers on a bus topology were connected to a single backbone cable. The computers all share this cable to transmit to each other, and each message is divided into frames. All the nodes (computing devices) receive all the data frames transmitted by any node. Each node then has to determine if the frame is to be accepted, using its unique identifier. Only one computer can successfully transmit at any one time, which is fine most of the time if the network is not too busy, but if there is a lot of traffic, collisions between data frames may occur and computers then have to retransmit. As the number of collisions increases, the network slows down.

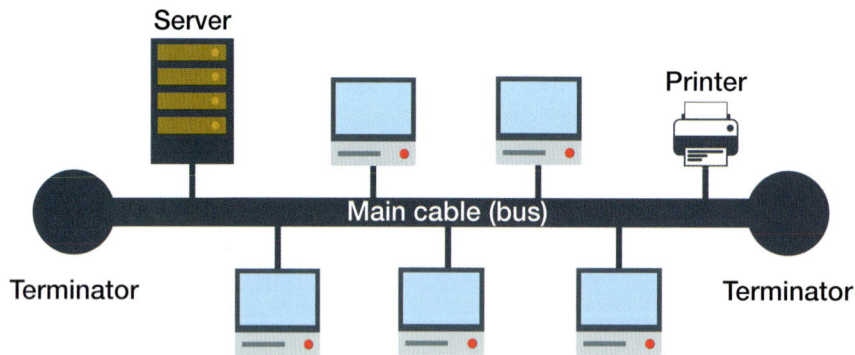

Advantages	Disadvantages
Easy and inexpensive to install – less cabling than in a star topology	If the main cable fails then the whole network goes down
No reliance on a central node	Cable failures are hard to isolate because all of the computers in the network are affected
	Performance slows down as the amount of traffic increases
	Low security as every node can see all the transmissions

A bus topology of this kind is a good choice for a temporary network in a single room, since it can be easily constructed with a minimum of cabling and extra hardware, and easily dismantled.

Mesh networks

A **mesh network** can be a local area network (LAN), a wireless LAN (WLAN) or a virtual LAN. Wireless mesh networks are an emerging technology, which can connect small offices or entire cities.

In a wireless mesh network, there is no central connection point. Instead, each point on the network acts as a 'node', equipped with a small radio transmitter. Information travels from node A to node B by hopping wirelessly from one mesh node to another, choosing the quickest route.

To connect to the internet, only one node needs to be physically connected via a modem. This node shares its connection with all the other nodes close to it. These nodes then share the connection with the nodes closest to them, and so on. The more nodes, the further the connection spreads, creating a wireless network that can serve a small office or a city of millions.

In a **full mesh network**, each node is connected to every other node.

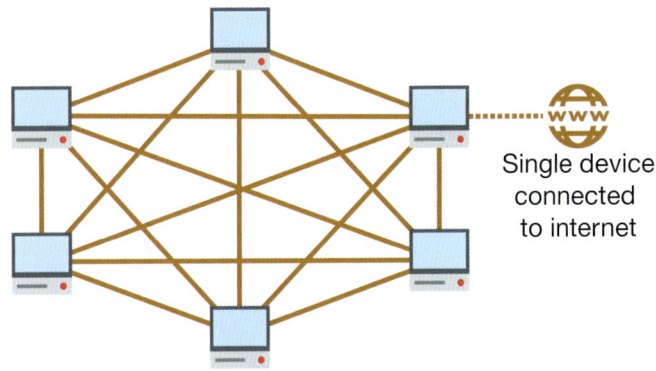

Single device
connected
to internet

In a partial mesh network, some nodes are not directly connected.

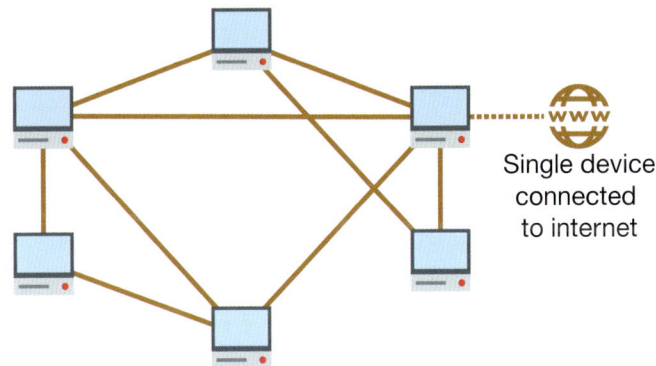

Single device
connected
to internet

4

The advantages of wireless mesh networks include:

- Using fewer cables means it costs less to set up a network, particularly over a large area of coverage
- The more nodes that are installed, the bigger and faster the wireless network becomes
- New nodes are automatically incorporated into the network without needing any adjustments by a network administrator
- Even if one node is blocked or faulty, the network will automatically 'self-heal' to find another route to send messages from one computer to another
- Local networks run faster because local packets don't have to travel back to a central switch or server

The disadvantages of wireless mesh networks include:

- Equipment such as a mesh router is more expensive.
- If a mesh cannot talk to one node, it will hop to another. This adds a slight delay in the communication.

4.5 – Network security

Networks are more vulnerable to hackers than standalone devices since a hacker may access a network through one device in order to gain access to other devices on the same network. This could have serious implications for an organisation, resulting in data theft, corruption of data, denial of service, and other damage caused by malware being installed on networked devices and servers. Network Security is important to prevent unauthorised access to data and misuse or modification of data.

Identifying network vulnerabilities

Penetration testing

Penetration testing is used to find any security weaknesses in a system. The strategy is to:

- gather information about the target of possible attacks
- identify possible entry points
- attempt to break in
- report back the findings

An **external penetration test** could target e-mail servers, web servers or firewalls. The objective is to find out whether a hacker can get in and, once they're in, how far they can get and what they can do on the system.

An **internal penetration test** puts the tester in the position of an employee with standard access rights, to determine how much damage a disgruntled or dishonest employee could cause.

> **Q4** Name some possible weaknesses or vulnerabilities that might be identified by:
> (a) an external penetration test
> (b) an internal penetration test

Ethical hacking

Hacking is the term used for gaining unauthorised access to data or a computer system. There are different types of hacker.

- **Black hat hackers** are those traditionally pictured in films and television programs. They gain access to computers illegally. They will have malicious intentions. For example, they may use the data for financial gain or cause damage to the system.
- **White hat hackers** are those involved in ethical hacking. They will have permission to carry out their hacking attempts. They will use similar methods to black hat hackers, however, a company or organisation will pay them to attempt to carry out the hacking. Any vulnerabilities will then be reported.
- **Grey hat hackers** are between black and white hat hackers. They typically try to find vulnerabilities in a system and do not have malicious intentions. However, they don't have permission to carry out their hacking attempts. Some grey hat hackers will report vulnerabilities they find, whilst others won't.

Ethical hacking is where a hacker has permission to attempt to carry out an attack on a company or organisations systems. They will remain within the limits the company has specified and report any vulnerabilities to them.

Methods of protecting networks

User access levels

User access levels should be set for drives, folders and files so users can only access what they need to. At school you can probably read files on a shared area but not edit them; this is Read-Only access. The teacher will have Read-Write access to these folders. Some folders you won't even be able to see.

In a work environment, the Accounts staff will have access to payroll details but other departments will not. The Data Protection Act says that employers must keep personal data secure so setting appropriate access rights is a legal responsibility.

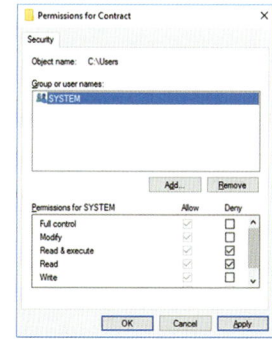

Firewalls

A computer connected to the internet is potentially accessible to anyone else on the internet. If a local area network, such as a school network, is connected to the internet then all the file servers, the email server, the web server and all computers on the network are potentially accessible. Some people hack 'just because they can' but often it is for identity theft or, for example, to get at bank account details and steal money. Occasionally people hack with malicious intent to disrupt or destroy files or entire computer systems but this is less common.

A **firewall** is designed to prevent unauthorised access to or from a private network. All messages entering or leaving the private network pass through the firewall, which examines each message and blocks those which do not meet specified security criteria.

Criteria may include for example:

- Where the access is from (the computer's address)
- The type of traffic (e.g. .exe files which may carry viruses)
- Specific web site addresses

A firewall doesn't just stop unwanted access from the outside world via the internet; it can also stop computers on a network from accessing specific sites or categories of site on the network. This feature is used to stop staff in companies watching the cricket while they should be working, or from using social networking sites during working hours. In school you'll find that many sites have been blocked. Try going to a games website or getting to Facebook on a school computer and you will probably get a message saying that the site has been blocked. It is the firewall software acting as a proxy server that stops this traffic getting out of the local area network and onto the internet.

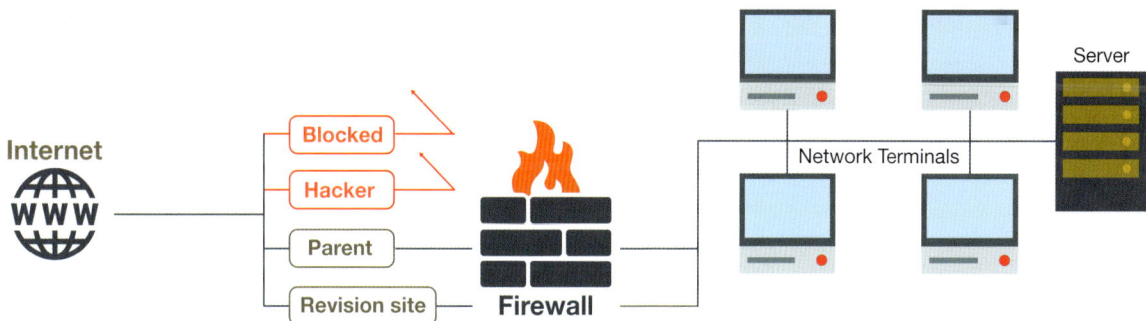

4

Operating systems such as MS Windows have firewall utilities included but you can also buy firewall software separately. Free firewall software can also be downloaded from the internet and some banks provide free firewall software to customers using their internet banking services.

Physical security

Physical security is important for every organisation.

- Security may start at the perimeter of the premises, with a barrier which can only be opened either by a guard or by entering a PIN or other ID.

- Security locks at the entrance which can only be unlocked by authorised personnel, including a receptionist to allow visitors to enter, are in common use.

- Barriers between the reception area and the rest of the building prevent unauthorised access.

- Servers are usually contained in locked rooms and locked cabinets.

Q5 Describe other physical security measures that may be implemented to prevent attacks on computer systems and networks.

Q6 Create a table with column headings

Prevention method   **What it may prevent**   **How it limits the attack**

Now complete the table for each of the methods of protecting networks given in the last two pages.

Exercises

1. A small company with five employees has installed a Local Area Network (LAN).

   (a) Describe what is meant by a Local Area Network (LAN). [2]

   (b) The network has been connected using a star topology.
   Describe the star topology. You may use a diagram. [2]

   (c) State **one** other item of hardware that is needed to connect stand-alone computers in a LAN, and briefly describe its purpose. [2]

   (d) Give **two** advantages and **one** disadvantage of connecting standalone computers in a LAN. [3]

   (e) The company is organising a week-long exhibition at a large exhibition hall. They need to set up a temporary local area network (LAN).
   State, with reasons, what type of LAN you would recommend. [3]

   (f) Draw a diagram of the bus topology. [2]

2. (a) A wireless network can be set up using Wi-Fi connections. What is Wi-Fi? [1]

   (b) Give **two** advantages and **two** disadvantages of wireless networks compared with wired networks. [4]

3. (a) Describe, with the aid of a diagram, the essential features of a mesh network. [3]

   (b) Give **three** advantages of a wireless mesh network. [3]

4. (a) When two computers on a network communicate, they have to use the same protocol. Define the meaning of the term protocol. [1]

   (b) State which would be the most suitable protocol in each of the following situations.
   Select one in each case, from the following: HTTP, HTTPS, FTP, IMAP, SMTP

      (i) Making a payment securely when purchasing something over the internet. [1]

      (ii) Transferring a file to another computer on a local area network. [1]

      (iii) Sending an email from one server to another server. [1]

   (c) Complete the table below to show which protocols operate on each of the layers given:
   TCP, IP, HTTP, FTP, SMTP, IMAP

Layer	Protocol
Application	
Transport	
Internet	
Link	

[7]

5. (a) Explain the purpose of **penetration testing**. [2]

   (b) Describe **two** different types of penetration testing. [4]

Section 5

Issues and impact

5

Objectives

- Understand environmental issues associated with the use of digital devices including energy consumption, manufacture, replacement cycle and disposal

- Understand ethical and legal issues associated with the collection and use of personal data including privacy, ownership, consent, misuse and data protection

- Understand ethical and legal issues associated with the use of artificial intelligence, machine learning and robotics including accountability, safety, algorithmic bias, legal liability

- Know the methods of intellectual property protection for computer systems and software including copyright, patents, trademarks and licencing

- Understand the threat to digital systems posed by malware including viruses, worms, Trojans, ransomware and keyloggers

- Know how hackers exploit technical vulnerabilities including unpatched software, out-of-date anti-malware and the use of social engineering to carry out cyberattacks

- Be able to describe the methods of protecting digital systems and data including anti-malware, encryption, acceptable use policies, backup and recovery procedures

5.1 – Environmental issues

Environmental issues associated with digital devices

The use of digital devices has many associated environmental issues. These include:

- Energy consumption
- Manufacture
- Replacement cycle
- Disposal

Energy consumption

All digital devices require energy to use. Desktop computers may typically consume 200 watts of power when running. Meanwhile, a more efficient laptop might require only 50 watts. Even more efficient tablet computers may require just 20 watts.

This energy usage almost always comes from the National Grid and therefore will contribute to the use of oil, gas and nuclear materials.

Most people are aware that computers and devices use energy, and as such they may choose more energy efficient devices and appliances. Domestic appliances, in particular, make use of energy efficiency labels to help inform customers and motivate them to buy more energy efficient models.

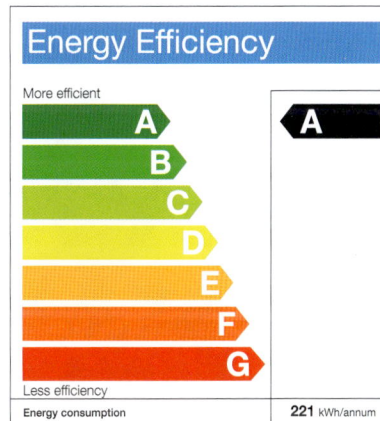

Manufacture

There are also significant amounts of energy required to manufacture electronic products. For instance, a desktop computer's manufacture could require the same amount of energy as running the computer in an office for over three years.

Computers and other digital devices make use of many different minerals such as iron, aluminium, copper, cobalt and cadmium. Even gold is used for the contacts on CPUs. These materials are not renewable, and if they cannot be recovered in recycling then they deplete reserves. The mining process itself may be harmful to the environment, wildlife and people.

Replacement cycle

The replacement cycle is the amount of time it takes from purchasing an electronic product to when it is replaced. Think about the energy use in the manufacture of a desktop computer. If the computer is used for just three years this would be significant. However, if the computer is used for nine years, only one third of the energy would have been needed for each year. The same can be said for all the raw materials that went into its manufacture.

As such, careful consideration should be made to using computers and digital devices for longer rather than discarding them when slightly newer models become available.

Replacing a laptop's hard disk drive

Disposal

When computers or electronic devices reach the end of their life they need to be disposed of. These items are classed as Waste Electrical and Electronic Equipment (WEEE). These items should not be sent to landfill and should instead be sent to recycling facilities. Be aware that not all components can be recycled and this also requires energy to carry out. It is better for the environment to increase the replacement cycle than make use of recycling and then purchase a new electronic device.

Q1 How could the replacement cycle of a smartphone or laptop be extended when the following happens?

(a) The screen is cracked.

(b) A fully charged battery no longer holds its charge for very long.

(c) The device has no more storage space to store photos and files.

Q2 Research the materials that go into the manufacture of an electronic product that you own.

Write down the findings from your research.

5.2 – Ethical and legal issues

Personal data issues

Personal data is any data that can be linked to you as a person. It includes obviously personal details such as your name, address and date of birth. It also includes sensitive data such as medical records and information about disabilities. Other personal data includes bank records, browsing history, email, text messages and exam results.

The Data Protection Act 2018

This Act contains a set of key principles that must be followed by all organisations holding personal data. It is designed to protect people's personal data. These are the principles of the Act:

- **Fair, lawful, and transparent processing**. Personal data must be processed lawfully and fairly for the purpose it was acquired, and with the individual's consent.
- **Purpose limitation**. Data must only be collected for specified, explicit and legitimate purposes.
- **Data minimisation**. Data must be adequate, relevant and not excessive, and must not be retained longer than necessary.
- **Accuracy**. Data must be accurate and up-to-date.
- **Data retention periods**. Data must not be retained longer than necessary. In addition, if a person asks for it to be erased, it must be securely deleted or destroyed.
- **Data security**. Data must be kept secure. This includes protection against unauthorised or unlawful processing and against accidental loss, destruction or damage.
- **Accountability**. Data controllers must be able to prove that their data protection measures are sufficient. Appropriate technical and organisational measures must be in place.

Privacy and consent

Personal data, and much more, may be stored on computers belonging to organisations such as schools, hospitals and social media companies. These organisations must respect people's **privacy**. They must make sure that the data is stored securely and only shared where it has been agreed it can be.

When someone agrees to their data being stored or processed, they give their consent to these uses. Most organisations require personal consent to use and store personal data. For example, a user will need to agree to the company's terms and conditions when signing up to a social media platform or an online shopping website. There are some exceptions where consent isn't required. For example, when the police investigate a crime, they don't need the permission of a criminal in order to process their information.

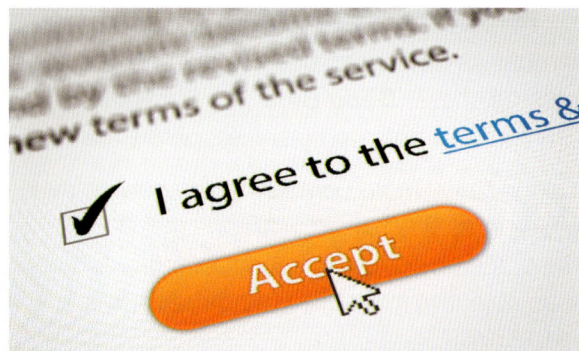

Data ownership

Data ownership refers to both those who are in possession of the data and those who are responsible for it. For example, a marketing company may have a list of customer names and email addresses. They own this data set. They are able to use and analyse the data. They can also sell the data if they have permission from their customers. At the same time, each of the customers are able to request that their data be corrected or removed from the mailing list.

Case study: Cyber-attack on Dixons undetected for nine months

In January 2020 Dixons Carphone was fined £500,000 (the maximum fine when the attacks took place) for breaches of the Data Protection Act. The personal details of customers were collected by means of malicious software installed on its 5,390 tills in Currys PC World and Dixons Travel chains.

The card details of more than five million customers were harvested as well as the full names, postcodes and email addresses of about 14 million people, leaving them exposed to increased risk of fraud. The malicious software went undetected for nine months between July 2017 and April 2018.

The Information Commissioner's Office said it had found "systemic failures" in the way Dixons looked after its customer data.

Maximum fines were increased in 2018, and in the summer of 2019, British Airways was fined £183m and the Marriot hotel chain £100m for breaches of the General Data Protection Regulation (GDPR).

5 Artificial intelligence and machine learning

Artificial Intelligence

Artificial intelligence (**AI**) enables computers to simulate human intelligence. These are pre-programmed 'behaviours' and have uses such as language translation, self-driving cars, speech recognition and non-playable characters (NPCs) in computer games.

For years, computer companies have been developing software programs to take on human opponents in games such as chess. **Deep Blue** was the first chess-playing computer to beat a world champion in 1996 when it defeated Gary Kasparov, the reigning world champion.

Go is a Chinese game significantly more complex than chess, played by millions of people all over the world. It is played on a 19 x 19 grid, with one player placing black stones and the other placing white stones, the object being to control more territory than your opponent. Until 2016, it had long been an objective in the field of artificial intelligence (AI) to develop software to beat a human champion.

Case study: DeepMind AlphaGo program

In March 2016 world champion Go player Lee Sedol from South Korea was defeated by Google's DeepMind AlphaGo program. This was the first time a computer had been able to beat a human player at the game.

The program taught itself how to improve by splitting itself in half and playing millions of matches against itself, learning from each victory and loss. In one day alone, AlphaGo was able to play itself more than a million times, gaining more experience than a human player could in a lifetime.

The co-founder Demis Hassabis said he hoped to use the same technique to help Google improve its products, such as its phone assistants and search engine. "The software learns by trial and error, incrementally improving and learning from its mistakes so that it makes better decisions."

In 2019, Lee SeDol retired from the game because machines could not be defeated. By that time, the machines had developed much further - a self-teaching version of the algorithm beat its predecessor 100 games to zero.

Machine learning

Machine learning is one way in which artificial intelligence can be achieved. Algorithms which are able to learn from training data are used. As more training data is given, the machine learning software is able to steadily improve its abilities.

Machine learning is a powerful technique that has resulted in many useful technological products in the last few years. For example, AI generated:

- photos and graphics
- essays and marketing copy
- computer code

Safety issues and accountability

Many artificial intelligence systems have learnt for themselves using machine learning techniques. This often means that no-one can fully understand how they are working. Unlike humans, machines don't have morals, so will run code, and carry out tasks without the ability to question themselves. This can lead to **safety issues**.

Self-driving cars are already being tested on Britain's roads, but what of the legal issues? Will the car be able to distinguish between a fox, a child or a plastic bag and make the appropriate decision about what action to take?

It is hard to work out who has **accountability** if a problem occurs. This makes determining legal liability (working out who to take to court) much harder. If someone is hurt or killed by a driverless car, who is to blame? The manufacturer, the owner of the car, or the person in charge of the car at the time?

> **Q3** What are the benefits and drawbacks of driverless cars?

Algorithmic bias

Artificial intelligence and machine learning may be used in ways that are biased. For example, search engine results have in the past been altered to promote a particular page by applying many links to the page. Equally, those creating the search engine algorithms may have their own biases which cause results not to appear in a fair order of relevance.

Machine learning algorithms may make use of learning materials which have biases in them against a particular gender, ethnicity, political view or other characteristic.

For instance, if an AI system were asked to create a written speech about a situation, the political bias may create viewpoints that aren't fair, correct or neutral. Corrections to bias may be added to the software, however, these themselves may carry biases.

> **Q4** Predictive policing tools allow police to be deployed where there are more reports of crimes from victims. How could these types of tools have algorithmic bias and negative consequences?

Robotics

Robots in films and television programmes often are human looking. However, they have many uses beyond this portrayal. For instance, in car manufacture, six-axis robots are used in welding, assembly and moving parts. The robotic arm is able to rotate and move across six degrees of freedom (ways in which the arm moves or rotates). Medical robots may help surgeons to carry out procedures or allow them to operate from remote locations. Meanwhile, domestic robots can now undertake tasks such as vacuum cleaning or mowing the lawn.

> **Q5** What safety risks could there be in working with robots in industry? How could these risks be reduced?

> **Q6** What risks could a companionship robot have when talking to the elderly as compared with a family member or carer?

Intellectual property

Intellectual property refers to any products or ideas that are created using the mind. It includes stories, inventions, photos, logos and computer code.

Copyright and patents

Copyright is designed to protect the creators of **works** such as books, music, videos and software from having their work illegally copied. Copyright protection is automatically given to any works as they are created. There is no need to apply for registration. Copyright lasts for a certain period of time after which the work can legally be copied. For instance:

- Written and musical works last until 70 years after the author or composer's death
- Sound and music recordings last for 70 years after being first published
- TV broadcasts last for 50 years after being first broadcast

The copyright symbol © is used on works to help show that the work is copyrighted. It appears alongside the year and author or publisher.

Patents are ideas that have an inventive step. Patents must be registered and a fee paid. Patents must be renewed every 5 years and can last up to 20 years. The principal of patents is that they protect inventors' and companies' ideas so that they can exploit them without competitors using them. In exchange, the public gain access to how the idea works and anyone can use it for free after 20 years. Companies will often buy licences so that they can use ideas developed by others that are still under patent.

The Copyright, Designs and Patents Act 1988

This Act makes it illegal to use, copy or distribute commercially available software without buying the appropriate licence.

If you buy a music CD or pay to download a piece of music, software or a video, it is illegal to:

- pass a copy to a friend
- make a copy and then sell it
- use the software on a network, unless the licence allows it.

The software industry can take some steps to prevent illegal copying of software:

- The user must enter a unique key before the software is installed
- Some software will only run if the CD is present in the drive
- Some applications will only run if a special piece of hardware called a 'dongle' is plugged into a USB port on the computer.

5

Trademarks

A trademark is a symbol, word or phrase which is used to name or give an identity to a product, company or service.

Unregistered trademarks make use of the symbol ™, whilst registered trademarks use the ® symbol.

Q7 Name the three symbols used to show that:

(a) a product name, that has been registered, can't be used by competing products

(b) a book cannot be copied

(c) a phrase, that hasn't been registered, is used by a company as part of their marketing of a product

Software licences

A software licence is a licence agreement giving permission to an individual or an organisation to use a piece of software such as a suite of programs for word processing, accounts, or another specialised application.

It is usually illegal to buy one copy of a program and copy it to multiple computers (see **proprietary software** below). Instead of buying multiple licences, an organisation may buy a site licence which allows the software to be copied to a specified number of computers.

Open Source software is governed by the Open Source Initiative that says:

- Software is licensed for use but there is no charge for the licence. Anyone can use it.
- Open Source software must be distributed with the source code so anyone can modify it.
- Developers can sell the software they have created.
- Any new software created from Open Source software must also be 'open'. This means that it must be distributed or sold in a form that other people can read and also edit.

This is different from **Freeware** (free software) which may be free to use but the user does not get access to the source code. Freeware usually has restrictions on its use as well.

Proprietary software is sold in the form of a licence to use it.

- There will be restrictions on how the software can be used, for example the license may specify only one concurrent user, or it may permit up to a certain number of users on one site (site licence).
- The company or person who wrote the software will hold the copyright. The users will not have access to the source code and will not be allowed to modify the package and sell it to other people. This would be a breach of copyright under the Copyright, Designs and Patents Act (1998).

5.3 – Cybersecurity

Cyber security consists of the processes, practices and technologies designed to protect networks, computers, programs and data from attack, damage or unauthorised access. It is defined as the protection of computer systems, networks and data from criminal activity. Cybercrime can take many forms, including planting viruses, acquiring and using personal or confidential data and disrupting a website or service.

Vulnerability of a computer network is often due to a flawed system which is open to attack. An attacker or hacker can then exploit this weakness.

Malware

Malware is the term used to refer to a variety of forms of hostile or intrusive software, some of which are described below.

Viruses

A **virus** is a program that is installed on a computer without your knowledge or permission with the purpose of doing harm. It includes instructions to replicate (copy itself) automatically on a computer and between computers.

Some viruses are just annoying and don't really do any damage but others will delete and / or change system files so that work files are corrupted or the computer becomes unusable. Some viruses fill up the hard drive / SSD so that a computer runs very slowly or becomes unresponsive.

How are viruses spread?

- Viruses are often spread though attachment to emails or instant messaging services. The recipient may be invited to open a funny image, greetings card, audio or video file.
- They may also be spread through files, programs or games that are downloaded from a web page or by loading an infected file from a USB stick or a CD/DVD.

> **Q8** A new DVD containing games software is bought from a known manufacturer. Explain why is it unlikely that this will contain a virus?

Worms

A worm is a type of malware that aims to replicate and spread to other computers on a network or the internet. Worms don't need a user interaction (such as opening an email or inserting a USB stick) in order to replicate. They will use system and network resources when replicating which may lead to services slowing and financial loss to remove the worm.

Case study: The Morris worm

The first worm was the 1988 Morris worm. The worm made use of vulnerabilities in several operating system programs and weak passwords. It replicated quickly and was able to infect many computers multiple times.

It is estimated that it infected 60,000 computers, roughly 10% of the internet at the time. The cost of removing the worm was around $10 million.

Trojans

A **Trojan**, named after the famous Ancient Greek story of the Trojan Horse, is a program which masquerades as having one legitimate purpose but actually has another. It may be spread by an email. The recipient is invited to click on a link for some routine or interesting purpose, which then executes a program which may, for example, give the controller unauthorised access to that computer. Alternatively, the Trojan may be placed inside proprietary software. The user is enticed to download it as the software will be free and have the registration security removed. Once installed, the Trojan horse can run in the background.

The motives vary – the Trojan may crash the computer, show pop-up advertising, spread malware across the network, corrupt data or reformat drives or access sensitive information.

Ransomware

Ransomware is malware which encrypts hard drives and other storage devices. Once encrypted, it reveals to the user that they need to pay a fee to unencrypt the data. It is usually impossible for the user to retrieve the data without paying the fee.

The ransomware gives the user a time limit to pay the fee. If they don't pay, the data will be deleted. This method adds urgency to the user's decision.

Often the value of the lost data is higher than the fee to recover it, making it financially worth paying. However, police usually advise not to pay as this encourages further ransomware attempts to be made.

If the user or organisation has backups of the drives then the data can be recovered. However, even this method results in lost time restoring devices.

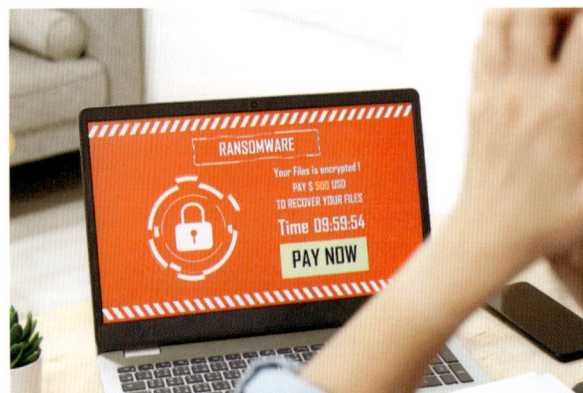

Key loggers

Key loggers log every key pressed on a keyboard. They may be installed as malware or may use a hardware dongle (small device that fits into a USB port).

By logging every key pressed, passwords can be revealed as they were typed. This information may then give a hacker the ability to log into the computer and other online sites where the password has been entered.

Some websites ask for only particular letters from a password to be entered. This helps reduce the effectiveness of using key loggers as the hacker won't have the full password, nor will they know the position of each letter entered.

Technical vulnerabilities

There are more technical vulnerabilities which may affect computers. These include:

- Unpatched software
- Out-of-date anti-malware
- Social engineering

Many of the risks of these technical vulnerabilities can be significantly reduced by an organisation's security policies, training and good management of computer systems.

Unpatched software

Software companies selling software such as operating systems, browsers, commercial applications packages and games are very alert to the possibility of their software being attacked by malware. Most vulnerabilities are 'patched' within 24 hours of being discovered. However, although users may be notified and offered a free software update, not every organisation or individual will automatically take up the offer leaving themselves open to attack.

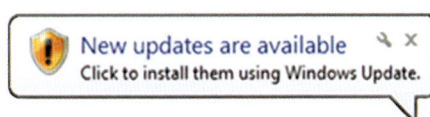

> **New updates are available** ⚊ ✕
> Click to install them using Windows Update.

Q9 An operating system asks the user to run an update. Explain the security risk that is created if the update is not run.

Out-of-date anti-malware

Anti-malware includes **antivirus** software. More about this type of software is given on **page 64**. This software makes use of virus and malware signatures to determine whether software or a computer is infected. It frequently has to update its malware database in order to detect new types of malware.

Out-of-date anti-malware will leave the computer open to attacks from certain viruses and other malware.

Social engineering

People are often the weakest point in security systems, and criminals have engineered methods to take advantage of human error and gullibility. It doesn't matter how many burglar alarms and double locks you have installed in your home, if you believe the robber who comes to the door and says he is there to check the electric meter.

Social engineering is the art of manipulating people so they divulge personal information such as passwords or bank account details. It is much easier to pretend to be trustworthy, and to fool an acquaintance or colleague into telling you personal information, than to try to secretly hack into their computer to find it out.

Social engineering includes the following techniques:

- blagging
- phishing
- shouldering (shoulder surfing)

Blagging is the act of 'knowingly or recklessly obtaining or disclosing personal data or information without the consent of the controller' (owner of the data). For example, a dishonest employee may persuade a colleague to tell them private information such as their password, pretending that they need it in order to install some new software on their computer. This then gives them access to their computer files and could lead to a security breach or even identity theft.

Shouldering or **shoulder-surfing** refers to using direct observation techniques to gain information such as passwords or security data; for example, looking over someone's shoulder while they type in their PIN or password.

In a crowded place such as a high street or an airport, it may be relatively easy for someone to watch you as you type in a PIN or password.

Phishing is when an attacker tricks someone into giving sensitive information, taking inappropriate action, such as making a phone call to ask for a manager's password or installing malware.

For instance, an email may request that someone opens an attachment containing important financial information. When they open the attachment, malware is installed. This is a phishing attack as the person was tricked into opening the attachment.

An alternative common phishing attack is to have a link in an email. If the link is opened, it may ask the user to enter personal details, such as for a bank log in. Once obtained, the hacker can then use these details to log in to the actual bank website as the user.

Q10 Describe **one** other way you might recognise a 'phishing' email. How can you protect yourself from falling for a phishing attack?

Protection methods

Anti-malware software

Anti-malware software will protect a computer in three ways:

- It prevents harmful programs from being installed on the computer
- It prevents important files, such as the operating system, from being changed or deleted
- If a virus does manage to install itself, the software will detect it when it performs regular scans. Any virus detected will be removed if it matches one in the malware database.

Anti-malware software will contain a database of virus and malware definitions. These are used to detect if files, that have been downloaded or are about to be run, contain malware.

If malware is detected, it will be quarantined and prevented from being run. The user can then delete any infected files.

New viruses are created regularly so it is important that any anti-malware software gets regular updates from the internet.

Encryption

Anything transmitted over a network can be intercepted and read. This is especially true for Wi-Fi networks, but also true with cabled networks if someone has access to the cables or switches. Interceptions usually take place without leaving any trace, so nobody knows they have happened.

One way of stopping this unauthorised access to data is to encrypt anything sent on a network. Encryption changes the data before it is transmitted so it can only be deciphered by someone with the appropriate key. To anyone intercepting the message it would be unintelligible.

When you buy something on the internet or use internet banking you may have noticed that instead of HTTP in front of the domain name it changes to HTTPS. It works in the same way as HTTP but is encrypted so your payment details are kept secure.

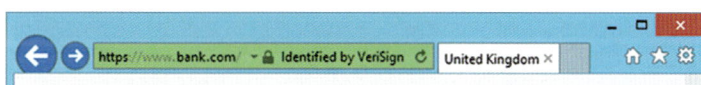

Acceptable use policies

Organisations such as companies and schools need to clearly explain to all users, such as employees, teachers and students exactly what behaviours are and are not accepted when using their computer systems. These policies also are likely to explain how data is used.

An acceptable use policy may contain requirements of users such as:

- Not telling anyone else their password
- Not logging into anyone else's computer account

Q11 Look at the acceptable use policy for your school. What other requirements and information does it give?

Acceptable use policies are also used for websites. Here they may also be called **terms of use** or **terms of service**. By using the website, users will be agreeing to these terms.

Backups and recovery procedures

It is important that computer systems and data are **backed up** frequently. Firstly, this should be carried out in case of drive failure. Secondly, it is also important to back up as some malware may delete files or drives. Ransomware, in particular, encrypts whole drives so that the user cannot gain access to their data. If frequent daily backups are made, they will only lose up to one day's worth of work if such an attack occurs.

Backups may be used to **restore** individual files or entire drives or file servers. For more information about backups **see page 63**.

Backups are typically made to external disk drives or tape drives due to their cheaper storage costs. These will be stored at an external location which helps protect against damage from fire or flood. Alternatively, the data may be stored on remote backup servers or cloud storage on the internet.

5

Recovery procedures need to be carefully thought about before a disaster or cybersecurity attack occurs.

For example, if a backup is stored offsite, the length of time needed to transport a backup to the office in order to restore the data will need to be considered. In some cases, such as fire, the time needed to purchase and deliver new hardware may also be a factor for consideration.

For some incidents, such as a failed hard disk, there may be spares located on the premises so that data can be restored quickly.

Care should be taken when considering recovery procedures and how long it will take to restore systems.

Q12 A company uses cloud storage to backup their file server. They have lost 1 TiB of data due to a fire in the server room. They plan to restore the data to their spare server. The cloud backup service allows them to download the backup data at 24 Mbps. How long will it take to download the data to restore the file server?

Exercises

1. A company purchases a desktop computer for use in an office.

    (a) Describe **two** ways that the manufacture of the desktop computer impacts the
         environment.   [2]

    (b) The company currently has a replacement cycle of three years.

         (i)   Define what is meant by replacement cycle.   [1]

         (ii) Explain **one** way that the environmental impact of the desktop computer could
               be reduced.   [2]

2. A company makes use of artificial intelligence and machine learning when selecting which
    people applying for a job should be interviewed.

    (a) Define what is meant by artificial intelligence in this situation.   [1]

    (b) Describe how machine learning could be used in this scenario.   [2]

    (c) Describe how algorithmic bias could be a problem when artificial intelligence is used to
         choose the people who will be invited for an interview.   [2]

3. HairTech have created a new innovative product for drying hair.

    They want to protect their new idea and the marketing that goes with it.

    (a) In the table below, tick the appropriate way to protect each different aspect of intellectual
         property.

HairTech intellectual property	Legal protection that HairTech could use		
	Registered patent	**Registered trademark**	**Copyright**
The innovative way in which the product works			
The computer code used to make the company's website			
The name of the product			

[3]

    (b) HairTech is concerned by the risk of malware such as key loggers on their computer
         systems.

         (i)   Explain how a key logger would be a threat to their computer systems.   [2]

         (ii) Give **two** other types of malware.   [2]

    (c) Describe a suitable backup procedure for HairTech.   [3]

Section 6A

Programming basics

Objectives

6A

- Know the function of, and be able to identify constants, variables, initialisation, assignment, sequences, selection, repetition, iteration, data structures and input/output.

- Be able to write programs that make use of sequencing, selection, repetition and iteration.

- Be able to use both count-controlled and condition-controlled loops.

- Be able to iterate over every item in a data structure.

- Write programs that make appropriate use of primitive data types including integer, real, Boolean and char.

- Use one-dimensional and two-dimensional structured data types including string, array and record.

- Write programs that make use of variables and constants.

- Be able to write programs that manipulate strings including length, position, substrings and case conversion.

- Be able to write programs that accept and respond appropriately to user input.

- Be able to write programs that read from and write to comma-separated value text files.

- Write programs that use arithmetic operators including addition, subtraction, division, multiplication, modulus, integer division and exponentiation.

- Be able to write programs that use relational operators including equal to, less than, greater than, not equal to, less than or equal to, and greater than or equal to.

- Write programs that use logical operators AND, OR and NOT.

Python

The programming language used for Edexcel Paper 2 is **Python** (version 3). The exam board produces a **Programming Language Subset** (**PLS**) which you should use as a reference when programming. This covers all the different parts of Python that could be used to solve problems and answer questions in the Paper 2 exam.

Python is a free programming language and may be downloaded from **https://www.python.org/downloads/**

6A.1 – Data types and operators

Variables, data types and constants

Any data that a program uses must be stored in main memory locations, each given its own identifier while the program is running. As the program runs, the values in these locations might change, which is why they are called **variables**. For example: a variable called `total` might change several times as many numbers are added to it. A variable called `surname` may change as the program processes a list of customer orders.

Each variable has an **identifier** (a unique name) that refers to a location in memory where the data item will be stored. Each variable also has a **data type** that defines the type of data that will be stored at the memory location and therefore the operations that can be performed on it (for example, you can multiply two numbers but you can't multiply two words).

Data types

Variables need to be declared before they are used. In some languages, such as C# or Java, you need to state what type the variable will be. In Python, the variable type is determined by the value it is first given. So if you write `a = 23`, `b = "Fred"`, `a` will be stored as an integer (whole number) and `b` will be stored as a string (text).

The table below shows the different data types that are used in Python.

Data type	Data type in Python	Meaning	Example of the data type being used
Integer	int	A whole number, positive or negative.	`age = 15`
Floating point number	float	A number with a decimal point.	`height = 1.73`
Boolean	bool	Holds the value True or False.	`gameOver = True`
String	str	A sequence of one or more letters.	`city = "Leeds"`
Character	str	One letter. In Python this is held in a string.	`firstInitial = "S"`

6A

Assignment statements

Values are assigned to variables using an = sign. For example:

```
x = 1
pi = 3.142
alpha = "a"
street = "Elm Street"
over18 = True
```

The first time that a variable is given a value it is **initialised**.

Constants

In some programs, there are certain values that remain the same (constant) while the program runs. The programmer could use the actual value in the code each time, but it is good practice to give the value a unique name (an **identifier**) and then use that name throughout the program. **Constants** are declared at the start of a program and can then be referred to as needed in the code. Python doesn't have constants. However, uppercase letters separated by an underscore character are used to show indicate that a variable is being used as a constant.

At the start of the program: **VAT_RATE** = 0.2;

Later in the program code: sellPrice = netPrice * **VAT_RATE** + netPrice;

The two main benefits of declaring a constant are:

- To change the value in the program, you only have to edit it in one place rather than looking for every place in the program where you used that value
- The code will be easier to read and understand because the constant's identifier will be used instead of a number. This makes your code easier to debug and, later on, maintain.

Input and output

Example 1

Write pseudocode for a program that asks the user to input their name. It should accept a name, for example 'John' and then display 'Hello John' on the screen.

```
myName = input("Please enter your name: ")
print("Hello " + myName)
```

The first statement displays on the screen

```
Please enter your name:
```

and waits for the user to enter something. If the user types John, the print statement then displays on the screen

```
Hello John
```

The first statement could be written as two separate statements:

```
print("Please enter your name: ")
myName = input()
```

However, you can generally use one statement to display a prompt and accept user input.

The second statement uses **concatenation** to join two strings together.

Concatenation symbol

```
print("Hello " + myName)
```

Alternatively, print statements can use commas to output text and variables. For example:

```
print("Hello", myName)
```

Operations on data

Operations are things you can do to specific types of data. For example, you can perform arithmetic operations on numbers and you can perform string-handling operations on text.

Numerical data types

Operations that can be performed on numerical data types are as follows:

Arithmetic operations *(give a numerical result)*		**Comparison operations** *(give a boolean result: true or false)*	
eg: 25 + 3 = 28		eg: 456 > 34 is true	
+	(addition)	<	(less than)
-	(subtraction)	>	(greater than)
*	(multiplication)	<=	(less than or equal to)
/	(division)	>=	(greater than or equal to)
**	(exponentiation)	!=	(not equal to)
//	(integer division)	==	(equal to)
%	(modulus)		

6A

The // operator means integer division in Python. It works like normal division but returns the whole number of times one number goes into the other. Here are some examples:

```
13 // 3 = 4
30 // 3 = 10
32 // 3 = 10
```

The % operator means modulus in Python. It gives the remainder after integer division has taken place. For example:

```
13 % 3 = 1
30 % 3 = 0
32 % 3 = 2
```

The exponentiation operator calculates the power of a number, so for example `7**2 = 49`

Q1 State the values of w, x, y and z that will be output when these statements are executed:

```
w = 54
x = w % 7
y = x // 2
z = y**3
print(w, x, y, z)
```

Type conversion

There are situations when you will need to convert from one data type to another. This is done with functions such as `int()`, `float()` or `str()`.

Changing a string to an integer

You may need to convert a string to a number so that you can use it in a calculation.

In Python, all user input is accepted as a string. If it contains a number that is needed in a calculation it will need to be converted.

Consider the following program:

```
num1 = input("Please enter first number")
num2 = input("Please enter second number")
num3 = num1 + num2
print("The sum is ", num3)
```

If the user enters 3 and 5, you would expect `num3` to be 8. However, the program outputs:

```
The sum is 35
```

What has happened? The numbers are input as strings, and the + symbol when used with strings means concatenation, or joining the two strings together.

You need to convert each of the strings to integers or floating point numbers. A corrected program would look like this:

```
num1 = int(input("Please enter first number"))
num2 = int(input("Please enter second number"))
num3 = num1 + num2
print("The sum is ", num3)
```

The `int()` function changes the variable type to an integer.

The `float()` function changes a string variable to a floating point number:

```
price = float(input("Please enter price: "))
```

> **Q2** Write a program which asks the user to enter a first name and surname, and prints out the whole name.

Changing an integer to a floating point number

If you divide an integer by another integer, and end up with a floating point number, Python will automatically convert the result to a floating point number for you. However, in a programming language which requires you to declare variables and their types before using them, you should declare the result of a division as a floating point (real) number.

```
num1 = 10
num2 = 3
num3 = num1 / num2
print(num3)
```

will print `3.33333333333333` or something similar.

In summary: (Note the use of quote marks to define strings.)

```
str(27)        returns    "27"
str(4.7)       returns    "4.7"
int("27")      returns    27
float("5.67")  returns    5.67
bool("True")   returns True
```

> **Q3** Write a program that asks the user to enter the total amount of a restaurant bill, divides it by 5 and prints out what each person owes.

String manipulation

A string is anything enclosed in quote marks. Programming languages have built-in functions to manipulate strings.

The functions below are given in a Python format. Each programming language will have its own particular functions and syntax.

String length

To get the length of a string:

```
len(stringname)
```

Position

Individual letters are obtained from a string by using their index.

```
string[index]
```

For example:

```
Message = "Hello"
print(message[1])
```

This will output the letter 'e'. Python string indexes start at position 0, not 1. This means that `stringname[0]` contains the first character of a string called `stringname`.

Substrings

A **substring** is part of a string. In Python, extracting a substring is carried out using string **slicing**. To find a substring in Python use the syntax:

```
string[start:end]
```

For example:

```
message = "Hello everyone"
substring = message[4:8]
print(substring)
```

The output will be "o ev". This is because position 4 in the string contains "o" and positions 5, 6 and 7 contain " ev". Remember space is included as a position in the string. The end position isn't included in Python.

To get the first characters from a string use:

```
string[:end]
```

For example, `message[:8]` will result in "Hello ev".

To get the last characters from a string use:

```
string[start:]
```

For example, `message[start:]`

For example, `message[11:]` will result in the substring `"one"`.

> **Q4** Write a program that asks the user to enter their full name, then output the first three letters in the name, followed by three dots.

Substring position

It is possible to find the position of a substring by using

```
string.find(substring)
```

The position will be returned. If the substring isn't in the string then -1 will be returned.

For example:

```
message = "Hello everyone"
position = message.find("very")
print(position)
```

This will return the position 7 as the 'v' in `"very"` is in index 7 in the string.

Case conversion

To convert cases:

```
string.upper()
string.lower()
```

For example:

```
message = "Hello everyone"
print(message.lower())
print(message.upper())
```

This will return:

```
hello everyone
HELLO EVERYONE
```

Repeating characters

In Python, it is possible to repeat a string by using * followed by the number of times the string should be repeated.

For example:

```
underline = "-+-"*10
print(underline)
```

This will output: -+--+--+--+--+--+--+--+--+--+-

Example 2

In the statements below, the result of each operation is shown in a comment on the right. In the pseudocode that we will be using, all comments will start with the hash symbol #.

```
myName = "John Robinson"
firstname = myName[0:4]                    # "John"
surname = myName[5:]                       # "Robinson"
numChars = len(myName)                     # 13
lastTwoChars = myName[len(myName)-3:]      # "on"
lastTwoChars = myName[-2:]                 # "on"
positionOfRob = myName.find("Rob")         # 5
```

Q5 Write a program to assign the number 5387026 to an integer variable. Convert this to a string, and print out the number of digits in the integer, followed by a comma, followed by the middle three digits. The output for this number would be `7,870`.

Q6 Write a program to accept a first name and surname from the user, which may be entered in lowercase or uppercase. Print the initials in uppercase, separated by a space.

Every character is represented in binary, for example using the ASCII representation. ASCII, "A" is represented by the same binary code as the decimal number 65, "B" is 66, "C" is 67,... "Z" is 90.

The functions ord and chr convert characters between ASCII and decimal.

```
num = ord("A")     # makes num = 65
letter = chr(66)   # makes letter = "B"
```

6A

Q7 Write a program to accept a character from the user, convert it to uppercase, and output the next character in the alphabet.

Other useful string functions

The following string functions are also available in Python. You should be aware of how these work as they are included in the Edexcel PLS.

String function	Description	Example

`string.isalpha()`	Checks if the string contains alphabetic letters. If it does then it returns True.	`message = "Southampton"`
		`print(message.isalpha())`
		
		`Output: True`

`string.isalnum()`	Checks if the string contains alphanumeric letters and numbers A-Z and 0-9. Returns True if that's all it contains.	`message = "Southampton23"`
		`print(message.isalnum())`
		
		`Output: True`

`string.isdigit()`	Returns true if the string contains just digits 0-9.	`message = "498"`
		`print(message.isdigit())`
		
		`Output: True`

`string.replace(string1, string2)`	Replaces all occurrences of string1 with string2.	`message = "Southampton"`
		`print(message.replace("South",`
		`                      "North"))`
		
		`Output: Northampton`

`string.split(character)`	Splits a string on each occurrence of the character. Each substring is stored in a list.	`message = "Lemon,Apple,Peach"`
		`fruitList = message.split(",")`
		`print(fruitList)`
		
		`Output: ["Lemon", "Apple",`
		`         "Peach"]`

`string.strip(character)`	Remove all occurrences of the character from the string.	`message = "...Beach.."`
		`print(message.strip("."))`
		
		`Output: Beach`

`string.isupper()`	If all the characters in the string are in uppercase then it returns True.	`message = "HELLO"`
		`print(message.isupper())`
		
		`Output: True`

`string.islower()`	If all the characters in the string are in lowercase then it returns False.	`message = "hello"`
		`print(message.islower())`
		
		`Output: True`

`string.index(substring)`	This works in the same way as `string.find(substring)` which was discussed earlier. The difference is that it raises an exception (rather than returning -1) if the substring isn't found. Use this only if you are using exceptions.	

String formatting

Sometimes when outputting text, you want to format the appearance. This is particularly important when creating tables of information.

`string.format()` is used to format the output of text.

For example, a wholesaler wants to show a list of products they have in stock:

```
tableLayout = "{:<10} {:<5d} {:6.2f}"
print(tableLayout.format("Bread", 207, 1.893))
print(tableLayout.format("Milk", 112, 1.591))
print(tableLayout.format("Chocolate", 349, 3.978))
```

The output from this code is:

```
Bread      207     1.89
Milk       112     1.59
Chocolate  349     3.98
```

Let's look at how the code works.

```
tableLayout = "{:<10} {:<5d} {:6.2f}"
```

This line of code sets the format of each row.

< means align to the left. The alternatives are centre-align (^) and right align (>).

d stands for a decimal integer.

f stands for a fixed point number. The 6.2f means give this column 6 characters width with two decimal places. Notice how the number 3.978 has been rounded up to two decimal places.

Q8 The following code outputs three different underground lines along with their lengths in miles and the year they were opened.

Complete the first line of code of the following program so that the output matches the one shown.

```
tubeFormat = "                              "
print(tubeFormat.format("Central line", 46.0, 1900))
print(tubeFormat.format("Piccadilly line", 44.1, 1906))
print(tubeFormat.format("Victoria line", 21.0, 1968))
```

Output:
```
Central line     46   1900
Piccadilly line  44   1906
Victoria line    21   1968
```

6A.2 – Sequence and selection

In Section 1, the basic program structures of sequence, selection and iteration were briefly covered. In this section the use of these structures will be looked at in more detail, with examples of more complex algorithms.

Sequence

All programs have a series of steps to be followed in sequence. Here is an example in which the steps are simple assignment statements:

Example 3

```
score1 = int(input("Enter score for Round 1: "))
score2 = int(input("Enter score for Round 2: "))
print("The average score is " + str((score1 + score2)/2))
```

Selection

Before looking at algorithms using the different selection statements available in a programming language, we need to take a closer look at Boolean data types and expressions, since these are used to determine which path through the program will be taken.

Boolean data type

Boolean variables are either **True** or **False**. It makes no sense to perform mathematical operations on them or to compare them to see which is greater. With Boolean variables we use **logical operators** to create **Boolean expressions**. Suppose that A represents some condition, for example x <= 10, or speed > 30. Logical operations **and**, **or** and **not** may be used in Boolean expressions, where:

not: If A is True, then (not A) is False

and: If A is True and B is True, then (A and B) is True, otherwise (A and B) is False

or: If either or both of A and B is True, then (A or B) is True, otherwise (A or B) is False

Boolean expressions

Boolean expressions are used to control selection statements. For example:

```
if score > 30:
    print("Well done")
```

In Python, the colon at the end of the first line means THEN. The lines of code which are to be carried out are indented.

A complex Boolean expression contains one or more of the operators **and**, **or** or **not**.

For example:

```
if x <= 10 or currentCharNum > lengthOfString:
```

Consider an estate agent's program that searches through a file of house details to find ones that match a customer's requirements. In this case the customer wants a house or flat, but it must have more than three bedrooms:

```
if rooms > 3 and (type == "House" or type == "Flat"):
    # output details
```

Notice the set of brackets around the second half of the expression. AND takes precedence over OR so without the extra brackets the program would return all the houses with more than three bedrooms as well as any flats, whether they have more than three bedrooms or not.

If, elif and else

If statements allow code to be run if a condition is true. If the condition isn't true, then other conditions may be tried using elif (which stands for else if). If all the conditions are false, then an else statement can then be run.

Example 4

Consider a program that has different outputs depending on the day of the week entered:

```
if day == "Saturday":
    print("Go to the shops")
elif day == "Sunday":
    print("Relax")
else:
    print("Go to work")
```

Each **block** of code to be run is indented for each condition.

The elif and else statements are optional. As many elif statements may be added as you need. Only one else statement may be added, and it needs to be the last statement as it is run after all the if and elif statements are false.

Writing robust code

Robust code is code which will not result in the program crashing due to an unexpected user input. The pseudocode below would crash for some inputs. Why?

```
num1 = int(input("Enter first number: "))
num2 = int(input("Enter second number: "))
print(num1/num2)
```

The problem here is that if the second number entered is zero, the calculation number ÷ 0 will be attempted. This will cause a divide by zero error.

The algorithm needs to be amended so that it will not crash whatever the user enters.

```
num1 = int(input("Enter first number: "))
num2 = int(input("Enter second number: "))
if num2 == 0:
    print("Cannot divide by 0")
else:
    print(num1/num2)
```

Example 5

A room is to be carpeted using carpet that is 4m wide. The program asks the user to enter the room dimensions, and if both width and length are greater than 4m, prints out "Carpet not wide enough". Otherwise, it calculates the length of carpet required by adding 5% to the length of the room.

```
roomLength = float(input("Enter room length: "))
roomWidth = float(input("Enter room width: "))
if roomWidth > 4:
    print("Carpet not wide enough")
else:
    carpetLength = roomLength * 1.05
    print("Length of carpet required = " + str(carpetLength))
```

The algorithm could still give the wrong answer if the user entered a width greater than 4, and a length less than the width, as it assumes that the user always enters the shortest dimension as the width. The program needs to check for this. Here is the rewritten algorithm:

```
roomLength = float(input("Enter room length: "))
roomWidth = float(input("Enter room width: "))
if roomWidth > 4 and roomLength < roomWidth:
    temp = roomLength
    roomLength = roomWidth
    roomWidth = temp
if roomWidth > 4:
    print("Carpet not wide enough")
else:
    carpetLength = roomLength * 1.05
    print("Length of carpet required = " + str(carpetLength))
```

6A

Q10 How much carpet does the algorithm calculate is required if the user enters:

(a) a length of 2 and a width of 4?

(b) a length of 3 and a width of 5?

Q11 Write an algorithm to solve the following problem:

- If a student gets a level 9 in GCSE maths, he or she will be advised to consider taking Further Maths at A Level
- If a student gets a level 8 in GCSE maths, he or she will be advised to consider taking Maths at A Level
- If a student gets a level 7 in GCSE maths, he or she will be advised to consider taking Maths at AS Level
- Otherwise, they will be advised not to continue with Maths.

6A.3 – Repetition and iteration

Repetition means looping over a block of code a given number of times or whilst a condition is true. **Iteration** is very similar to repetition, but it is performed over every item in a data structure, for example, each letter in a string or each item in a list.

In Python, repetition and iteration are carried out using while and for loops.

The while loop

The expression in the while statement controlling the repetition must be a Boolean condition which evaluates to True or False.

The expression is tested at the **start** of the loop.

This means that sometimes the statements inside the loop are not executed at all. Boolean expressions are used to control this type of loop. For example:

```
reply = ""
while reply != "compScience":
    reply = input("Please re-enter password: ")
```

You may sometimes need complex Boolean expressions, for example:

```
while (not A > B) and (not ItemFound):
```

Q12 Write a program to allow a user three attempts to enter the correct password, "compScience".

A while loop is also useful when allowing a user to continue entering data until they indicate there is no more data to enter by inputting a "dummy" value. Here is an algorithm which allows a user to continue entering values until a dummy value of xxx is entered.

```
total = 0
markstring = ""
while markstring != "xxx":
    markstring = input("Please enter next mark, xxx to end: ")
```

```
    if markstring.isdigit():
        mark = int(markstring)
        total = total + mark
print("Total of all marks: " + str(total))
```

Q13 Write a program which allows a user to enter daily temperatures and when the user enters xxx, outputs the maximum and average temperature.

As while loops check a condition at the start of the loop, they are known as **condition-controlled** repetition.

The for loop

This type of loop is useful when you know how many times the loop is to be repeated. They are also referred to as **count-controlled** repetition.

For example, if you wanted to print out the numbers from 0 to 3 on the screen, you could use the following program:

```
for i in range(0,4):
    print(i)
```

The first line of code says that the value stored in the variable named i will be in range (0,4). Ranges don't include the final number, so i will take the values from 0 to 3 for each time the loop repeats.

The output from this program will be:

```
0
1
2
3
```

Q14 Write a program which outputs the 5 times table. The output should be:

1 x 5 = 5

2 x 5 = 10

...

10 x 5 = 50

For loops with step

Sometimes, a for loop may need to count in another number such as twos or threes. The range allows a step to be added. For example, to count to 10 in twos:

```
for i in range(2,11,2):
    print(i)
```

The output from this program will be:

```
2
4
6
8
10
```

To count down, use a negative step. For example, for a program that counts down from 4 to 1:

```
for i in range(4,0,-1):
    print(i)
```

The output from this program will be:

```
4
3
2
1
```

For loops in structures

For loops are able to iterate through the values in any structure, not just a range.

This is particularly useful in Python lists (covered on **page 117–119**). As a string is essentially a list of characters, Python can iterate across a string. For example, to output all the letters in a user input:

```
word = input("Enter a word: ")
for letter in word:
    print(letter)
```

The output from this program where the input is `'Hello'` will be:

```
H
e
l
l
o
```

The for loop here uses `letter` for the variable name. It could have used `i` as in previous for loops. However, `i` is usually only used when storing numbers that are used for the iteration. Using more meaningful variable names makes the code easier to understand and read.

Q15 Write a program which will ask the user to enter a word, then output each letter in the word on a separate line using the capital letter.

Q16 Write a program which will ask the user to enter a word. It will then translate each letter in the word to the next letter in the alphabet. Each letter will be output on a separate line. If the letter z or Z is encountered then the letter a or A will be output.

Nested loops

You can have one loop nested inside another.

Example 6

```
for table in range(2,13):
    for row in range(1,13):
        answer = table * row
        print(str(table) + " x " + str(row) + " = " + str(answer))
```

Q17 Adapt the program in Example 6 so that it asks the user how many tables and rows it should produce. For instance, if the user enters 5 tables and 10 rows then the program will output:

2 x 1 = 2

2 x 2 = 4

...

5 x 10 = 50

6A.4 – Arrays and lists

We have said that all the variables needed in a program are held in main memory. If we were processing one or two specific data items, then we would have a different identifier for each of these. For example, a program that adds two numbers together might use variables called `num1`, `num2` and `total`, all of type integer.

Often a program will process a number of data items of the same type, for example if it is sorting a list of 1000 student names.

We could use variables called `student1`, `student2`, `student3`, ... `student1000` to store the names but programming languages allow you to use an **array** to make processing groups of data easier to code. An array is a group of data items of the same data type, which is stored under one identifier (name) in contiguous (one after another) memory locations.

Python doesn't have arrays, but instead uses **lists**. Lists allow different items with different data types to be stored in them. They also allow items to be added to or removed from the list.

1-dimensional arrays (or lists in Python)

This program processes 12 numbers using a simple array of integers called `score`. Imagine a table with one row of 12 boxes:

Each box in the table can contain an integer. Each box has a numerical reference called an **index** that is used to refer to that individual data item. Note that the first element of the array shown here has an index of zero. For example, the third box in this array is referred to as `score[2]`.

The individual boxes in the array can be used just like variables:

- **Assign** values to them: `score[4] = 27`
- **Input** values into them from the keyboard or a file:

      score[4] = int(input("Enter score: "))

- **Output** the value stored in a box to the screen or a file:

      print("The fourth value is ", score[3])

The benefits of using arrays are:

- Code is easier to follow and therefore easier to debug and maintain
- A group of data items can be easily processed using a for loop

When you process data held in an array, you typically do the same thing to each data item, so having them stored in numbered locations makes this much easier and quicker to code.

Example 7

The following algorithm initialises each element of an array to zero, then gets 12 numbers from the user, adds them up and outputs the total:

```
total = 0
score = [0]*12
for game in range(0,12):
    score[game] = int(input("Enter number: "))
    total = total + score[game]
print("Total is " + str(total))
```

`score = [0]*12` creates a list named `score`. It is initialised with 12 zeros.

An alternative way to initialise a list would be:

```
score = [0,0,0,0,0,0,0,0,0,0,0,0]
```

An empty list (a list that contains nothing, but can be added to) is created using either one of the following lines of code:

```
listName = list()
listName = []
```

It is possible to add an item to a list with the code:

```
listName.append("Item")
```

Q18 Write a program which asks the user for ten names and inputs them into a list, converts each name to uppercase and prints out the list at the end.

2-dimensional arrays

Suppose you need to store 10 test scores for each of a class of 30 students. You could use a 2-dimensional array called `classScores`, which would, for example, hold the 4th test score for the second student in `classScores[1][3]`. (Remember the array indices start at 0.)

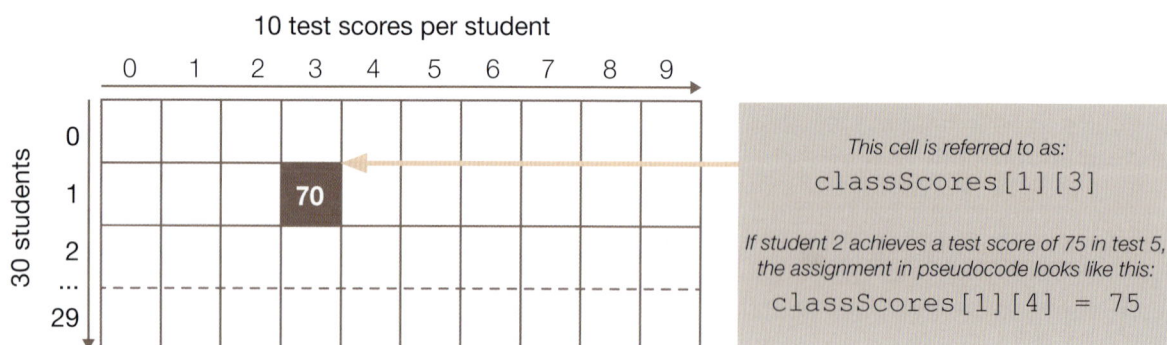

10 test scores per student

0 1 2 3 4 5 6 7 8 9

30 students

0
1 70
2
...
29

This cell is referred to as:
`classScores[1][3]`

If student 2 achieves a test score of 75 in test 5, the assignment in pseudocode looks like this:
`classScores[1][4] = 75`

Example 8

Write a program to allow the user to enter 3 test scores for each of 4 students. Calculate and print the average score obtained by each student.

The student names are held in an array `studentName` so that for example `studentName[0]` contains the name **Adams, Peter**. An array `total` will hold the total scores for each student.

```
#initialise arrays
total = [0,0,0,0]
average = [0,0,0,0]
#initialise array of student names
studentName = ["Adams, Peter", "Harris, Delia", "Mehmed, James",
               "Smith, David"]
#initialise 2-dimensional array
scores = [ [0,0,0],
           [0,0,0],
           [0,0,0],
           [0,0,0] ]
#input names and marks
for student in range(0,4):
    print("Enter 3 scores for ", studentName[student])
    for mark in range(0,3):
        scores[student][mark] = float(input("Enter score: "))
        total[student] = total[student] + scores[student][mark]
    for n in range(0,4):
        average[n] = total[n]/3
        print("Average for " + studentName[n] + " " +
              str(average[n]))
```

6A

Q19 Run the program above. The test data is entered as follows:

Adams, Peter has test scores of 6, 4, 5

Harris, Delia has test scores of 8, 7, 9

Mehmed, James has test scores of 6, 10, 8

Smith, David has test scores of 5, 3, 4

Show the final contents of the arrays `scores`, `total` and `average` when the program is run.

What is the value held in `scores[2][1]`?

Q20 Quarterly sales (in £000s) for each of six supermarkets are held in a two-dimensional array sales which has 6 rows and 4 columns. Write an assignment statement to assign the value 150 to Store 5 for the third quarter sales.

Other list functions

Two other useful list functions are:

```
del listName[5]                 Removes the item located at index 5.
listName.insert(5, "Item")      Adds "Item" into the list at index 5.
                                All other items move down the list by 1.
```

6A.5 – Records and files

Previously we looked at arrays. An array is a collection of data items stored under one identifier so that the data items can be processed easily. When we group data items together so they can be treated as a set of data, we refer to this as a **data structure**.

Records

Most languages will allow arrays to be defined quite easily but sometimes we want to define our own data structures. Imagine a program for a car sales showroom. If your program is going to process details about cars, it will be easier to create a record structure to hold all of the car details rather than storing them as one long string of text or lots of separate variables. We cannot put them in an array because the separate data items we need to store about each car are not all of the same data type.

Here is a text file with some car details in it:

```
RE05 HSD, Ford, 2005, 97500, 650
SW12 SDF, Vauxhall, 2012, 59650, 2500
BN64 WJR, Nissan, 2014, 39900, 18000
```

We could process this file as lines of text but it would be easier it we defined our own data type that gave this line of text some structure. Delphi is a high-level programming language. A Delphi programmer could define this record type as follows:

```
type TCar = record
   registration:   string;
   make:           string;
   year:           integer;
   mileage:        integer;
   price:          integer;
end;
```

Individual data items within a record are called fields.

Table: CarTable

registration	make	year	mileage	price
AV60 HES	Peugeot	2010	33156	£5,500
GF56 RTE	Toyota	2006	26875	£8,500
FD02 YOU	Hyundai	2002	85300	£3,499
AD62 HGF	Peugeot	2012	50887	£7,649
AF63 HTE	Peugeot	2013	45860	£6,780
GF64 NGB	Renault	2014	38665	£6,199
GR11 JUL	Renault	2011	90760	£2,999

In Python, records are not available. Instead, lists are used. Lists are able to store items with different data types which makes this use possible.

For example, to store the car table, a 2D list could be used as follows:

	0	1	2	3	4
0	AV60 HES	Peugeot	2010	33156	5500
1	GF56 RTE	Toyota	2006	26875	8500
2	FD02 YOU	Hyundai	2002	85300	3499

Example 9

The following example shows how the first three records could be added to the table. Then the user enters a car registration and new price. The car price is then updated for this car. The car table is formatted so that it appears like a table.

```python
allCars = []
car1 = ["AV60 HES", "Peugeot", 2010, 33156, 5500]
car2 = ["GF56 RTE", "Toyota", 2006, 26875, 8500]
car3 = ["FD02 YOU", "Hyundai", 2002, 85300, 3499]
allCars.append(car1)
allCars.append(car2)
allCars.append(car3)
carReg = input("Enter car registration: ")
newPrice = int(input("Enter new price: "))
for i in range(len(allCars)):
    if allCars[i][0] == carReg:
        allCars[i][4] = newPrice
tableLayout = "{:<10} {:<10} {:<10} {:<10} {:<10}"
for i in range(len(allCars)):
    print(tableLayout.format(allCars[i][0], allCars[i][1],
            allCars[i][2], allCars[i][3], allCars[i][4]))
```

Q21 (a) Update the program above so that it adds a fourth car with the details:

AD62 HGF, Peugeot, 2012, 50887, 7649.

(b) The program currently asks for the registration and the new price. Allow the user to also update the mileage of the car.

Handling text files

The pseudocode programs we have looked at so far have all used variables which are stored in memory. Often, however, the data needs to be stored in a **file** which can be held permanently on disk, from where it can be read next time it is needed.

Text files contain text that is in lines. There is no other structure, unlike files of records. When you read from a text file you can only read a whole line at a time. When you write to it, you can only write one line at a time.

There are three different modes that files can be opened in:

- Read mode – the contents of the file can be read, but no changes can be made to the file
- Append mode – new content can be added to the end of the file
- Write mode – data can be written to the file

When reading, writing or appending to files, the following process is undertaken in the computer code:

- Open the file (in read, append or write mode)
- Read, write or append each line of the file
- Close the file

Example 10: Writing to a file

In this example we ask the user to input names and then write them to a text file.

```
nameFile = open("names.txt", "w") # w opens in write mode
moreNames = True
while moreNames:
    name = input("Please enter name: ")
    if name != "xxx":
        nameFile.write(name + "\n")
    else:
        moreNames = False
nameFile.close()
```

When using the write() function, the text is simply added into the file. The **\n** is known as an **escape character** for a new line. It is treated as one character, but won't display in the file.

Example 11: Reading from a file

Now the names are stored in the file, we can read them back and print them out, or store them in a list where they could then be processed, for example.

```
nameFile = open("names.txt", "r") # r opens in read mode
for line in nameFile:
    print(line)
nameFile.close()
```

Example 12: Reading multiple lines from a file

It is possible to read all the lines from a file at once and put them into a list ready for later processing.

```
nameFile = open("names.txt", "r")
names = nameFile.readlines()
nameFile.close()
for i in range(len(names)):
    names[i] = names[i].strip("\n")
print(names)
```

Be aware that the list will likely contain \n characters. The example shows how these can be removed by using the strip() function.

Example 13: Appending to a file

This example allows an individual name to be appended to the end of an existing text file.

```
nameFile = open("names.txt", "a") # a opens in append mode
name = input("Please enter name: ")
nameFile.write(name + "\n")
nameFile.close()
```

Example 14: Appending a list of strings to a file

Sometimes, you may already have a list of strings which you want to append to a text file. In this case, there is no need to append each line separately. All the strings can be added using just one Python function. Remember that new line characters \n and spaces will need to be in the strings if you want them to be in the text file.

```
names = ["Amy\n", "Brian\n", "Charles\n", "Dorothy\n"]
nameFile = open("names.txt", "a")
nameFile.writelines(names)
nameFile.close()
```

Processing CSV files

Table data is often stored in files with each field separated by a comma and each record on a different row. These files are known as **CSV (comma-separated values)** files. For example, the first three records of the cars table would be stored as:

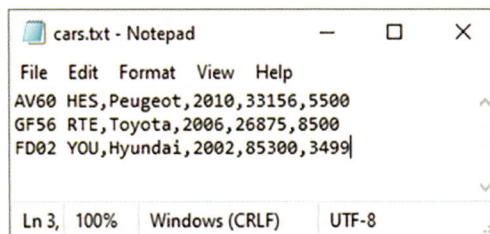

Example 15: Reading a CSV file

The following shows how the cars CSV file could be read and converted into a 2D list storing one car record on each row.

```
carTable = []
nameFile = open("cars.txt", "r")
for line in nameFile:
    line = line.strip("\n")
    carRecord = line.split(",")
    carTable.append(carRecord)
nameFile.close()
print(carTable)
```

The CSV file is first opened. Each line of the file represents one car record. So, for each line, first strip away any \n escape characters. Then split the line by the "," character. This creates a list of all the fields in the line. These are stored in the carRecord list. Now append this list to the carTable list. Finally close the CSV file.

Q22 Create a program which asks the user to enter the car details of car registration, make, year, mileage and price. Once entered, append this to a text file named `cars.txt`. Once the details have been entered, the program asks if the user wants to add another record. If so, it asks for the details again. If they don't, the program exits.

An example of the program's input and output:

```
Enter registration: AD62 HGF
Enter make: Peugeot
Enter year: 2012
Enter mileage: 50887
Enter price: 7649
Record added
Do you want to add another record? n
Program complete
```

This would store the following in the text file:

```
AD62 HGF, Peugeot, 2012, 50887, 7649
```

Exercises

6A

1. An integer 65 can be converted to a character using the statement:

   ```
   letter = chr(65)
   ```

   The ASCII value corresponding to the letter "A" is the integer 65, so this statement would assign "A" to letter.

   (a) Write a program which accepts three integers as input, and outputs the corresponding letters as one word. [4]

   (b) State the word that will be output if the user enters 66, 69 and 68. [1]

2. Fred has written a program to record temperature readings of a patient every hour for 6 hours and record the number of times the temperature is greater than 38, which is defined as an incidence of fever. His program is shown below.

   ```
   1  FEVER_TEMP = 38
   2  temp = 0
   3  hour = 0
   4  total = 0
   5  fever = 0
   6  while hour < 6:
   7      temp = float(input("Enter temperature: "))
   8      if temp > FEVER_TEMP:
   9          fever = fever + 1
   10     total = total + temp
   11     hour = hour + 1
   12 average = total / hour
   13 print("Average temperature: " + str(average))
   14 print("Incidences of fever: " + str(fever))
   ```

(a) State what is meant by a constant and give an example from the code. [2]

(b) State what is meant by a variable and give an example from the code. [2]

(c) Give **one** line of code where a variable is initialised. [1]

(d) Give **one** example of repetition in the code. [1]

(e) Explain why the function `float( )` is used in line 7. [2]

(f) Adapt the program so that it makes use of a FOR loop instead of a WHILE loop. [2]

3. (a) Write a program for an animal guessing game that does the following:
   - Assigns the word "cat" to a variable named answer
   - Assigns the user's input to a variable named guess
   - If the user correctly guesses "cat" then the program outputs "Correct", otherwise the program lets the user guess again
   - The game continues until the user guesses correctly [6]

   (b) Adapt the program so that it keeps a record of how many guesses the user has had. At the end of the game update the user with the number of guesses they took. [3]

4. A program has been written to count people as they enter a theme park ride. Each time the Return key is pressed, the onRide variable is increased by 1. When the onRide variable reaches 10 the program outputs that the ride is full. The program is shown below.

```
rideFull = False
onRide = 0
while not rideFull:
    if onRide < 10:
        input("Press return for another rider: ")
        onRide = onRide + 1
    else:
        rideFull = True
        print("Ride full")
```

6A

(a) Adapt the program so that the user can input any number of people to go on the ride.

The program should prevent a number being entered that would make the total number of people on the ride go over 10.
In this case the text "Not enough empty seats" should be output.

The user will always enter an integer. [5]

(b) Adapt the program further so that once the ride is full it then resets onRide back to zero ready to fill again. The program should continue looping in this way until 0 is entered. [5]

5. The following program uses two lists to hold the marks scored by five pupils in two Computer Science exams. It should compare the marks achieved by each student in the two exams, and print out, for example:

```
James score improved by 3
David score dropped by 5
```

Some extra statements in the program will be needed in the answers to the question. Note that array indexing starts at 0.

```
names = ["James", "David", "Isabella", "Sophie", "Ethan"]
score1 = [65, 66, 72, 66, 81]
score2 = [68, 61, 72, 69, 85]

for i in range(0,5):
    diff = score2[i] - score1[i]
    if diff >= 0:
        print(names[i] + " score improved by " + str(diff))
    else:
        print(names[i] + " score dropped by " + str(-diff))
```

(a) Adapt the program to:

    (i)   calculate and print the average mark obtained by each pupil over the two exams   [3]

    (ii)   calculate and print the average class score for each exam   [5]

(b) Save the name, score improvement and average mark for each pupil in a CSV text file. For example, the first two results would be in the text file as:

```
James,3,66.5
David,5,63.5
```
    [4]

Section 6B

Problem solving with programming

Objectives

- Be able to use decomposition and abstraction to analyse, understand and solve problems
- Be able to read, write, analyse and refine programs written in a high-level programming language
- Convert algorithms from flowcharts or pseudocode into programs
- Make programs easier to read, understand and maintain with the use of layout, indentation, comments, meaningful identifiers and white space
- Be able to identify, locate and correct program errors including logic, syntax and runtime errors
- Use logical reasoning and test data to evaluate a program's fitness for purpose and efficiency, including the number of comparisons, number of passes through a loop and the use of memory
- Understand the function of and be able to identify the use of subprograms and parameters
- Understand the need for and be able to write programs that implement validation, including length check, presence check, range check and pattern check
- Understand the need for and be able to write programs that implement authentication using an ID and password combination or lookup
- Be able to write programs that use pre-existing (built-in and library) and user-devised subprograms including procedures and functions
- Be able to write functions and procedures with and without parameters
- Understand the difference between and be able to write programs that make appropriate use of global and local variables

6B

6B.1 – Subprograms

A subprogram (also known as a subroutine) is a named, self-contained section of code that performs a specific task. It may return one or more values but doesn't have to.

Imagine a recipe for a lemon meringue pie. You could have the recipe written out in one long list of instructions but it might be easier to separate out instructions for making pastry and making meringue, especially as these same instructions will be used in several other recipes as well.

The recipe for Lemon Meringue Pie might say:

1. Make short-crust pastry (see Recipe 5)

2. Make the meringue (see Recipe 12)

3. Mix the lemon rind, sugar etc.

Programs are similar. If you have some code that does a specific task, it can be written as a self-contained subprogram. It can then be used from anywhere in the program as needed, without writing all the instructions out again and again.

In a system that has several parts to it, perhaps selected from a menu, it is much easier to write and debug your code if it is written in subprograms. The main program might be an IF statement that calls subprograms to process each menu choice:

```
displayMenu()
choice = selectOption()
if choice == 1:
    displayRules()
else:
    playGame()
```

In this example, a subprogram called `displayMenu()` is first called to display a menu of options.

Then a second subprogram, `selectOption()` is called which allows a user to select an option. The option selected is returned from the subprogram and assigned to a variable called choice.

Depending on the value of choice, either the subprogram `displayRules()` or `playGame()` is called.

You can see from this example that using subprograms makes the program structure really clear. Another benefit is that each subprogram can be written and tested in isolation from the other modules. This makes debugging much easier and, in the future, the program will be easier to maintain. Modules can also be reused in future programs.

Procedures

There are two different types of subprogram, called procedures and functions. We will look first at procedures.

Defining a procedure

This procedure prints a greeting.

```
def greeting():
    print("Hello")
    print("You're looking well")
```

To call this procedure, you write the name of the procedure wherever you want to call it.

```
greeting()
```

Nothing is returned from a procedure – it just carries out the instructions and goes back to the next instruction after the call statement.

Note that the keyword `def` stands for define. It is used to define both functions and procedures in Python.

Receiving information through parameters

To make the subprogram more useful, you can pass it one or more parameters. A parameter is a variable named in the subprogram heading that will receive and use whatever value you pass it.

```
def greeting(name):
    print("Hello " + name)
    print("You're looking well")
```

To call this subprogram, you write the name of the subprogram wherever you want to call it, and specify what parameter is to be used.

```
greeting("James")
greeting("Helen")
firstname = input("What is your name? ")
greeting(firstname)
```

When this program is run, it will print:

```
Hello James
You're looking well
Hello Helen
You're looking well
What is your name?
(user enters a name, e.g. Kerry)
Hello Kerry
You're looking well
```

You can pass as many parameters as you like, separated by commas.

Q1 Write a subprogram that accepts two parameters for oven temperature and number of eggs, and prints out, for example, "Set the oven to 180 degrees. You will need 3 eggs."
Write instructions to call the subprogram with two different sets of data.

Functions

Functions are similar to procedures; they are named, self-contained sections of code. The key difference is that they always return a value, using a RETURN statement.

We have already used several built-in functions such as chr() and ord():

```
letter = chr(68)           # assigns "D" to letter
asciiValue = ord("B")      # assigns 66 to asciiValue
```

Example 1

Here is a sample function to convert centimetres to inches. The function takes a parameter (input value) named cm.

```
def cmsToInch(cm):
    inches = cm / 2.54
    return inches
```

It could be used in a line of code like this:

```
heightInCM = float(input("Enter your height in centimetres: "))
heightInInches = cmsToInch(heightInCM)
print("Your height in inches is " + str(heightInInches))
```

The subprogram in this case contains a RETURN statement, which identifies it as a function rather than a procedure.

> **Q2** Write a function to accept two numbers and return the numbers added together. Test the function by calling it with the number 3 and 5. Output the result.

Local and global variables

A **global variable** is one which is declared in the main program and is recognised in all the subprograms called from the main program.

Functions and procedures may use their own **local variables** which are not known about or recognised outside the subprogram. In the function above which converts centimetres to inches, conversionFactor is a local variable, declared within the subprogram and only existing while the function is being executed. It is not recognised anywhere else in the program.

When a function or procedure is executed, it will automatically use the variables found locally, even if there is a global variable with the same name. If the variable is not found locally it will use the global variable. This means that the same variable identifiers can be used in several different procedures. This is useful if different people are writing different sections of the program.

Advantage of using local variables

- Using local variables in a subprogram is good practice because it keeps the subprogram self-contained. The subprogram can be used in any program and there will be no confusion over which variable names in the main program might conflict with names used in a subprogram.

- This also leads to the further advantage that the program will be easier to debug and maintain.

- If memory space is an issue, the use of local variables will save on memory as the space used by local variables is freed up when the subprogram completes.

Using local variables in a subprogram is a form of abstraction. The user of the subprogram needs only to know what inputs to the subprogram are required, and what the output will be. The detail of how the subprogram works and the variables it uses are hidden.

The following function returns the average of three numbers n1, n2 and n3.

```
def average(n1, n2, n3):
    total = n1 + n2 + n3
    avg = total/3
    return avg
```

The function could be called using the statement:

```
meanValue = average(5, 10, 15)
```

The return value, a local variable named `avg` in the subprogram, will be passed to the variable `meanValue` in the calling statement.

The variable `total` is also a local variable inside the function `average`. If you try to print it outside the function, you will get an error message.

Example 2

Here is an outline program written in pseudocode, with global and local variables declared. This is not normally done in pseudocode but is done here in order to illustrate the scope of variables.

```
theAnswer = ""
count = 0

def threeTimesTable():
    #local variables here
    count = 1
    while count < 6:
        print(count * 3)
        count = count + 1

#start of main program here
count = 33
threeTimesTable()
theAnswer = 10 * count
print("The answer is " + str(theAnswer))
```

`count` is declared globally at the start of the program.

`count` is also declared locally in the `threeTimesTable` subprogram.

Here the subprogram uses the local variable

Here the main program uses the global variable, which will hold a different value from the one declared in the subprogram

This is the output screen for this program.

```
3
6
9
12
15
The answer is 330
```

The program above would normally not use global variables with the same name as this is confusing. It has been written to illustrate local and global variables.

6B

Variables such as `count`, used to control loops, should always be local to that function or procedure. Even if you want to share data between subprograms, it is considered better practice to pass the data using parameters than to use global variables.

Local variables

- only exist while the subprogram is executing
- are only accessible within the subprogram

Q3 Study the program below and answer the questions.

```
def calcArea(radius):
    pi = 3.14
    area = pi * radius * radius
    return area
r = float(input("Enter the radius: "))
print("Area of the circle is " + str(calcArea(r)))
```

(a) Give an example of a local variable and a global variable in this algorithm.

(b) What will be the first statement to be executed?

(c) Identify the part of code that makes a function call.

(d) Identify the part of code that returns a value.

(e) Identify the part of code which is an argument for a function definition.

Example 3

Here is the same program as written earlier in Example 2. This time, it makes use of the global variable count. Compare the output with that in Example 2. Notice how the keyword `global` has to be used if you want to make use of a global variable inside a subprogram.

```
theAnswer = 0
count = 0

def threeTimesTable():
    global count
    count = 1
    while count < 6:
        print(count * 3)
        count = count + 1

#start of main program here
count = 33
threeTimesTable()
theAnswer = 10 * count
print("The answer is " + str(theAnswer))
```

This is the output screen for this program.

```
3
6
9
12
15
The answer is 60
```

6B

Q4 Complete the following trace table to show how the values change as the program is run. You will need 9 rows to complete the table.

theAnswer	count	output

Advantages of using subprograms

Using subprograms to perform specific tasks in a program has many advantages.

- Breaking down or **decomposing** a large problem into sub-tasks, and writing each of these as a subprogram, makes the problem easier to solve
- Each subprogram can be **tested** separately
- Subprograms can be used several times within a program
- Subprograms can be stored in a **subprogram library** and used in different programs if needed
- Several programmers can work on a large program at the same time, each writing different subprograms, so a large job will be completed more quickly
- If the requirements of a problem change, it is much easier just to make a change in a subprogram than to search through a long program to find what lines need changing, so program **maintenance** is easier.

6B.2 – Validation and authentication

Validating input data

Most programs require input from a user and so, in order to make sure the program will not crash or do something unexpected if the user enters a value that is not sensible or reasonable, all input data must be checked as soon as it is input. There are several types of **validation check** that can be carried out in a program:

- **Range check:** a number or date is within a sensible/allowed range
- **Type check:** data is the right type such as an integer, a letter or text
- **Length check:** text entered is not too long or too short – for example, a password is greater than 8 characters, a product description is no longer than 25 characters
- **Presence check:** checks that some data has been entered, i.e. that the field has not been left blank
- **Pattern check:** checks that the pattern of, for example, a postcode or email address is appropriate

Validation can only check if a data item is reasonable. It cannot tell if it is correct. This is an important difference. If a web form prompts for **Date of Birth**, the application can check that the data entered would be appropriate for that age group, but it cannot tell if you entered November instead of December by mistake.

Example 4 – Range check

The following algorithm asks the user to enter an integer between 17 and 30, and validates it by performing a range check. The number is then multiplied by 3 and the result printed out.

```
num = int(input("Enter number between 17 and 30:"))
while num < 17 or num > 30:
    num = int(input("Invalid number - please re-enter: "))
print(num * 3)
```

Example 5 – Type check

The following program asks the user to enter a number. It performs a type check. If the user has entered text rather than a number, they will be asked to enter the number again.

```
num = input("Please enter an integer: ")
while not num.isdigit():
    num = input("You must enter an integer, try again: ")
num = int(num)
print(num)
```

Other useful functions for checking the type of data entered include:

- `isalpha()`   Returns True if all the characters are alphabetic (A-Z)
- `isalnum()`   Returns True if all the characters are alphabetic (A-Z) or digits (0-9).

Example 6 – Length check

The following program asks the user to enter their name, and performs a length check. The name must be between 2 and 20 characters.

```
name = input("Please enter name: ")
while len(name) < 2 or len(name) > 20:
    name = input("Must be between 2 and 20 characters - please
re-enter: ")
print(name)
```

Q5 Write a program that asks the user to enter their first name. It then performs a presence check to see that they enter at least one character as the input. If they don't, it will continue to ask them to enter their name again.

Example 7 – Pattern check

A pattern check (also known as a format check) allows the checking of an email address, for example. Look at the following program which makes use of the split function to check that an @ symbol is in the address.

```
validEmail = False
email = ""
while not validEmail:
    email = input("Enter email address: ")
    emailParts = email.split("@")
    if len(emailParts) == 2:
        validEmail = True
    else:
        print("That isn't a valid email address")
```

The program splits the email address entered with each occurrence of the @ symbol. This should result in a list with two items, the left hand side and right hand side of the email address.

> **Q6** One problem with this program is that the left hand side and right hand side of the @ symbol could be empty, and this would still result in the program choosing it as a valid email.
>
> Adapt the program so that it checks to see there are characters before and after the @ symbol.

Authentication routines

Authentication of an individual is used to make sure that a person is who they say they are. **Biometric** methods could include optical, facial or fingerprint recognition.

Other methods include asking the user to enter a user ID and password. A simple identification routine is used when you log into a school network, or an online shopping site. Usually, you will be assigned a user ID and you choose a password when you first log in. The password is encrypted and saved in a file. When you enter your user ID and password, the password is encrypted and compared to the one stored for that user ID.

6B

> **Q7** Why are you normally only allowed three attempts to type in the correct password?

Example 8 – Authentication

The following screen shows how a username and password need to be entered for authentication of a user.

One solution to the authentication of a user is to have a table (2D list) which stores the username and password combinations.

Username	Password
hsmith	mRv2ab%9
agurund	45Pjz£kx
glaws	keoWP%$2

```
passwordList = []
passwordList.append(["hsmith", "mRv2ab%9"])
passwordList.append(["agurund", "45Pjz£kx"])
passwordList.append(["glaws", "keoWP%$2"])
validUser = False
while not validUser:
    username = input("Enter username: ")
    password = input("Enter password: ")
    for login in passwordList:
        if login[0] == username and login[1] == password:
            validUser = True
if not validUser:
    print("Incorrect password")
else:
    print("log in successful")
```

Once the user has entered their username and password, this combination is looked up in the `passwordList` table. Each username and password combination is checked to see if it matches what the user entered.

These passwords could be stored in a CSV file. In real life the usernames and passwords are usually stored in a database with the passwords encrypted.

Q8 Adapt the program above so that it only allows the user three attempts at entering the username and password. If they fail to log in within three attempts then output "account locked".

6B.3 – Developing code

When developing code, it is useful to make use of both decomposition and abstraction. These two concepts were covered earlier in Section 1.1.

Using decomposition

Take the development of a maths quiz game. The program could first be decomposed as follows:

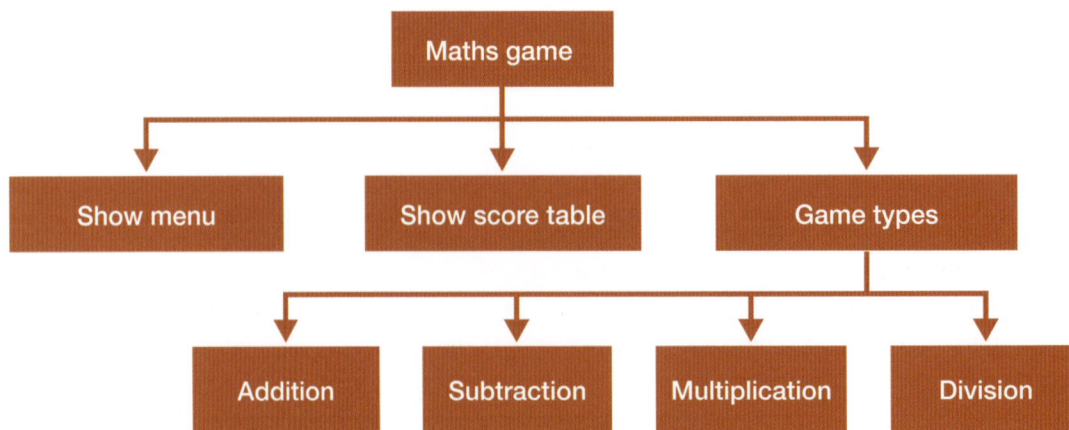

Breaking down the problem makes it easier for the programmer to solve each part. For instance, writing a program to show menu choices is much easier to understand than a program for an entire maths game.

Using abstraction

Example 9a

Using the decomposition diagram for the maths game, imagine that we are creating the different game types. We could make different subprograms to handle each of the four different question types.

For example, the subprograms for addition and subtraction questions could be written as follows:

```python
import random
score = 0

def additionQuestion():
    num1 = random.randint(0,9)
    num2 = random.randint(0,9)
    answer = num1 + num2
    question = str(num1) + "+" + str(num2) + "="
    userAnswer = input(question)
    if userAnswer == str(answer):
        return "Correct"
    else:
        return "Incorrect"

def subtractionQuestion():
    num1 = random.randint(0,9)
    num2 = random.randint(0,9)
    answer = num1 - num2
    question = str(num1) + "-" + str(num2) + "="
    userAnswer = input(question)
    if userAnswer == str(answer):
        return "Correct"
    else:
        return "Incorrect"

if additionQuestion() == "Correct":
    score = score + 1
if subtractionQuestion() == "Correct":
    score = score + 1
print(score)
```

There are two different subprograms for each type of question. These allow the programmer to use abstraction so that whenever a addition or subtraction question is needed, the programmer just calls the subprograms `additionQuestion()` or `subtractionQuestion()`.

Note that the statement `import random` imports the **random library** into a program. It is needed to generate the random numbers. This is an example of abstraction as the programmer doesn't need to know how the numbers are generated.

`random.randint(0,9)` generates a random number between 0 and 9. This is another example of abstraction as the programmer doesn't need to worry about all the details of how `randint` works.

> **Q9** Find the similar lines of code in `additionQuestion()` and `subtractionQuestion()`.

Example 9b

It is possible to take the parts that are common to both question functions and make a more general question function. The development of this function makes further use of abstraction.

```python
import random
score = 0

def mathsQuestion(questionType):
    num1 = random.randint(0,9)
    num2 = random.randint(0,9)
    if questionType == "+":
        answer = num1 + num2
    elif questionType == "-":
        answer = num1 - num2

    question = str(num1) + questionType + str(num2) + "="
    userAnswer = input(question)

    if userAnswer == str(answer):
        return "Correct"
    else:
        return "Incorrect"

if mathsQuestion("+") == "Correct":
    score = score + 1
if mathsQuestion("-") == "Correct":
    score = score + 1

print(score)
```

This solution has created a `mathsQuestion` function which is abstract. It can be reused for different maths operator questions, such as multiplication or division.

Q10 Adapt the program so that the function `mathsQuestion` also works for multiplication and division questions.

Converting algorithms into programs

Algorithms may be written in flowcharts or pseudocode. As a programmer, you need to be able to convert these algorithms into programs.

Converting flowcharts into programs

When converting flowcharts into programs, remember that certain symbols such as a decision box will change to an IF statement.

Loops in a flowchart will be implemented using a FOR or WHILE loop.

The following flowchart is used to find the top score from three scores.

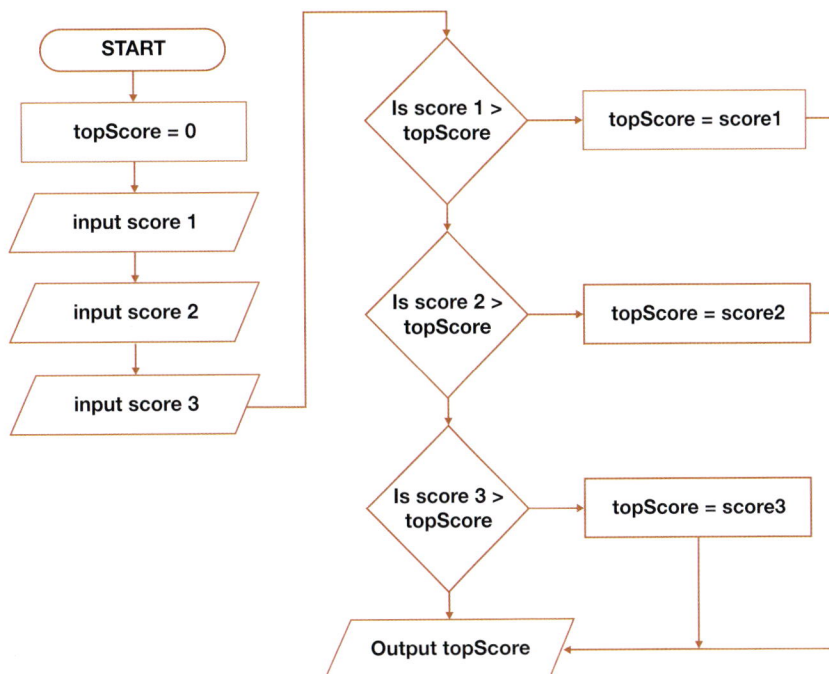

Convert the algorithm in the flowchart into a program.

Converting pseudocode into programs

6B

Pseudocode statements are less precise than programming ones. They should allow a programmer to understand how each part of the program works so that they can then convert it into a real programming language. Certain parts of the program, such as type conversion, may be ignored in the pseudocode as the programmer will understand that these need to be added to make the program work correctly.

```
classScores = []
totalScore = 0
WHILE moreClassScores:
    INPUT classScore
    append classScore to classScores
FOR i = 1 to classScores length
    totalScore = totalScore + classScores[i]
averageScore = totalScore / classScores length
OUTPUT averageScore
```

Q12 Convert the pseudocode above into a program.

Code readability

It is important for code to be readable as this helps both you and other programmers to understand and maintain it.

To make code more easily readable, make use of the following techniques:

- Use meaningful identifiers – for example, a list named `testScores` is far easier to understand than a list named `ts`.

- Code layout – declaring variables at the start of the program is one way to improve the layout. Having blank lines between code blocks also helps to make it easier to read and understand.

- Comments – comments are useful for helping to understand code. They don't need to be on every line as this is often unhelpful. They should explain difficult to understand lines of code or what the purpose of a function, procedure or block of code is.

- White space – using whitespace includes blank lines to separate code blocks, indentation of code blocks and using additional white space around operators – for example:

```
average = sum / total
```

is easier to read than:

```
average=sum/total
```

Q13 Look at the following code which calculates the maximum of two numbers. Rewrite the code to improve its readability.

```
def max(n1,n2):
    if n1>n2:
        return n1
    else:
        return n2
a=int(input("Enter first number: "))
b=int(input("Enter second number: "))
print("Larger number is: "+str(max(a,b)))
```

Errors and testing

When you write a program in a high-level programming language, a **translator** (**compiler** or **interpreter**, will scan each line of code and convert it into machine code. As you will already have found out, programming is not as easy as it looks.

- Firstly, it is very easy to make mistakes typing in the code, for example typing "prnt" instead of print. These are **syntax errors**.

- Secondly, once you have corrected all the syntax errors, the code may run but not do what you want. This means there are **logic errors** in your program.

- Thirdly, code may run, but create an error that crashes the program when it is running. These are known as **runtime errors**. For example, if a program tries to divide by zero.

Syntax errors

The translator expects commands to have a certain format, called syntax, just like a sentence in English has grammar rules. Syntax is a set of rules which defines the format of each command.

Example 12

The following example shows how a square could be drawn with the turtle.

Program	Output
```import turtle screen = turtle.Screen() screen.setup(800,400) turtle.screensize(800,400) turtle.speed(0) terry = turtle.Turtle() terry.forward(50) terry.right(90) terry.forward(50) terry.right(90) terry.forward(50) terry.right(90) terry.forward(50) terry.right(90) turtle.done()```	

Q21 Improve the code so that the square is drawn using a FOR loop.

Filling shapes

It is possible to have the turtle fill a shape with colour once it has been drawn.

The following subprograms are used:

Subprogram	Meaning
`terry.fillcolor("red")`	Change the fill colour to red. Alternatively, RGB colours can be used. For example (1, 0, 0) or "#FF0000" will also be red.
`terry.begin_fill()`	Start filling the shape.
`terry.end_fill()`	End filling the shape.

Q22 Create a program to draw a pentagon (five sided shape) that is filled with blue

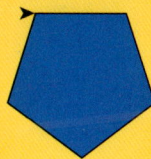

Turtle colours

Some predefined turtle colours include:

Blue, black, green, yellow, orange, red, pink, purple, indigo, olive, lime, navy, orchid, salmon, peru, sienna, white, cyan, silver and gold.

Other turtle subprograms

The following are additional subprograms that you are expected to understand with regards to turtles. The variable name of the turtle is again `terry`.

Subprogram	Meaning
`terry.mode("standard")` `terry.mode("logo")`	The standard mode is the default mode. The turtle will point east and angles are counterclockwise. If the turtle is set to logo mode then it will point north with angles being clockwise.
`terry.hideturtle()`	Hides the turtle.
`terry.showturtle()`	Shows the turtle.
`terry.pencolor("blue")`	Makes the pen colour the turtle draws with blue. Alternatively, RGB colours can be used. For example (0, 0, 1) or "#0000FF" will also be red.
`terry.pendown()`	Put the pen down. This makes the turtle draw.
`terry.penup()`	Lift the pen up. This stops the turtle from drawing.
`terry.pensize(5)`	Makes the pen thickness 5.
`terry.circle(50)`	Draws a circle of radius 50.
`terry.circle(50,90)`	Draws an arc of radius 50 and 90 degrees (one quarter of a circle).

Q23 Create a program to draw five different coloured hills like the ones below.

6B

Exercises

1. (a) The following program uses a function which accepts a time in hours, minutes and seconds and converts this to a number of seconds.

```
def timeInSeconds(hours, minutes, seconds):
    timeElapsed = (hours * 60 * 60) + (minutes * 60) + seconds
    return timeElapsed
```

Write one or more lines of code to call the function and print the time that has elapsed in seconds.

Test your program with 5 hours, 3 minutes and 42 seconds. [3]

(b) Write a procedure which accepts a person's age as a parameter. If the age is less than 17, display:

```
You cannot hold a full driving licence
```

Otherwise, display:

```
You are eligible for a full driving licence
```

Call the procedure with a user's input. [4]

2. The pseudocode below represents a function called `ArrayAverage`.

`ArrayAverage` is used to find the average of all the numbers stored in an array.

Note: line numbers have been shown but are not part of the function.

```
1 def listAverage(theList):
2     total = 0
3     for number in theList:
4         total = total + number
5     return total / len(theList)
```

6B

(a) State the number of parameters in the function `listAverage`. [1]

(b) This function uses iteration. Give the line number on which iteration starts. [1]

(c) The function uses variable assignment.

Give the line number in the function where variable assignment is first used. [1]

(d) Write one or more statements to call the function and output the average of the numbers in the array.

Use the list [3,2,5,10] to test your function. The average should be 5.0. [2]

3. A user is going to enter a car registration number into a program. The number should have the format:

    <letter> <letter> <number> <number> <space> <letter> <letter> <letter>

    For example, the registration number:

    AB12 CDE   would be valid.

    However,

    A12 CDE   would be invalid.

    (a) Write a program which will check if the user has entered a valid registration number.   [8]

    (b) Adapt the program so that it keeps asking the user to enter another registration number if they enter an invalid one.   [2]

4. The following program is used to have a turtle draw a house.

```
import turtle
screen = turtle.Screen()
screen.setup(800,400)
turtle.screensize(800,400)

turtle.speed(0)
houseTurtle = turtle.Turtle())

def drawHouse(turtle):
    turtle.pendown()
    for i in range(4):
        turtle.forward(50)
        turtle.right(90)
    turtle.left(45)
    turtle.forward(35)
    turtle.right(90)
    turtle.forward(35)
    turtle.penup()
    turtle.setheading(-90)
    turtle.forward(50)
    turtle.right(90)
    turtle.forward(18)
    turtle.pendown()
    turtle.right(90)
    turtle.forward(20)
    turtle.left(90)
    turtle.forward(10)
    turtle.left(90)
    turtle.forward(20)
    turtle.penup()
drawHouse(houseTurtle)
turtle.done()
```

    (a) Identify the line of code which calls the function drawHouse.   [1]

    (b) Adapt the program so that it creates a row of five houses.   [4]

Index

Clear**Revise** Guides
Multi-award-winning revision series

- Hundreds of marks worth of examination style questions
- Answers provided for all questions within the books
- Illustrated topics to improve memory and recall
- Specification references for every topic
- Examination tips and techniques
- Free Python solutions pack (CS Only)

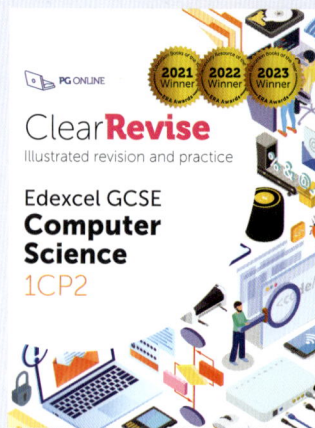

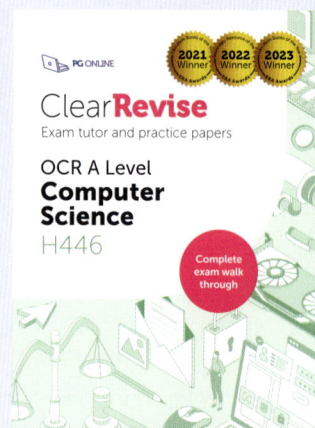

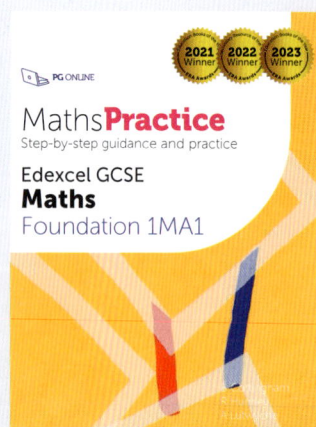

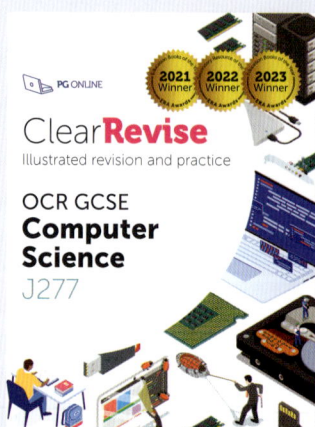

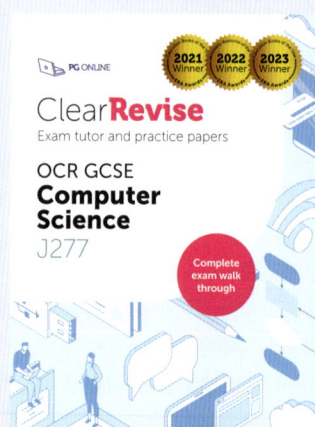

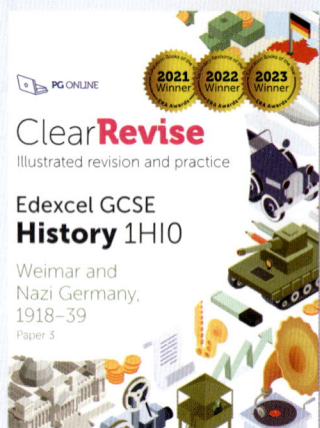

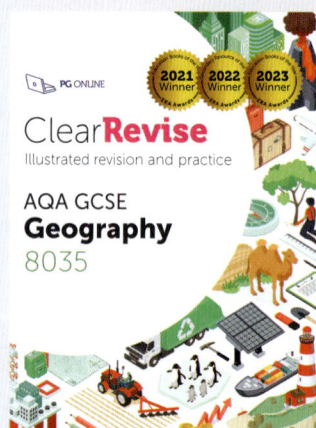

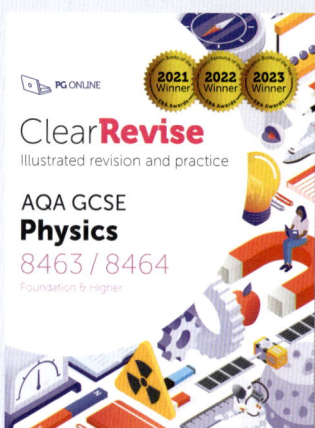

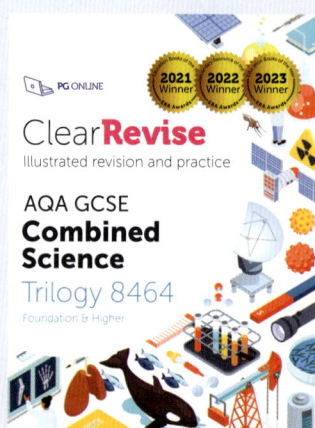

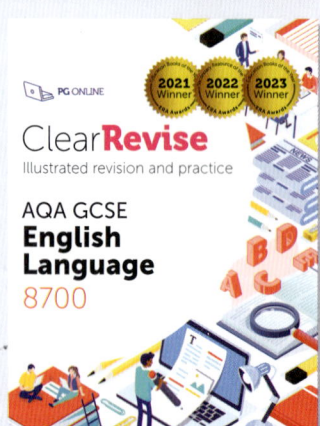

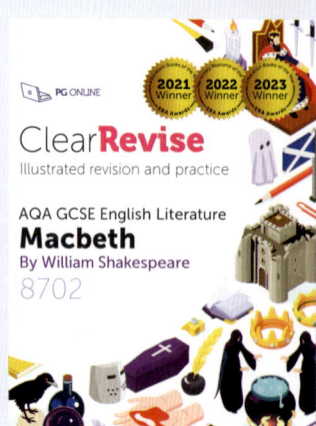

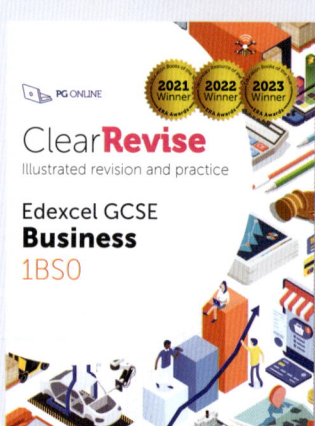

New titles coming soon!

Clear**Revise** — Illustrated revision and practice — Edexcel GCSE **Computer Science** 1CP2

Clear**Revise** — Exam tutor and practice papers — OCR A Level **Computer Science** H446 — Complete exam walk through

Clear**Revise** — Illustrated revision and practice — AQA GCSE **Design and Technology** 8552

Maths Practice — Step-by-step guidance and practice — Edexcel GCSE **Maths** Foundation 1MA1

Clear**Revise** — Illustrated revision and practice — OCR GCSE **Computer Science** J277

Clear**Revise** — Exam tutor and practice papers — OCR GCSE **Computer Science** J277 — Complete exam walk through

Clear**Revise** — Illustrated revision and practice — Edexcel GCSE **History** 1HI0 — Weimar and Nazi Germany, 1918–39 — Paper 3

Clear**Revise** — Illustrated revision and practice — AQA GCSE **Geography** 8035

Clear**Revise** — Illustrated revision and practice — AQA GCSE **Physics** 8463 / 8464 — Foundation & Higher

Clear**Revise** — Illustrated revision and practice — AQA GCSE **Combined Science** Trilogy 8464 — Foundation & Higher

Clear**Revise** — Illustrated revision and practice — AQA GCSE **English Language** 8700

Clear**Revise** — Illustrated revision and practice — AQA GCSE English Literature **Macbeth** By William Shakespeare 8702

Clear**Revise** — Illustrated revision and practice — BTEC Tech Award **Enterprise** Component 3

Clear**Revise** — Illustrated revision and practice — Edexcel GCSE **Business** 1BS0

Explore the series and add to your collection at **www.clearrevise.com**

Available from all good book shops

amazon | 𝕏 @pgonlinepub